HELPING YOUNG PEOPLE TO BEAT STRESS

Sarah McNamara

continuum
LONDON • NEW YORK

Continuum

The Tower Building
11 York Road
London SE1 7NX

15 East 26th Street
New York
NY 10010

First published as *Stress in Young People* 2000
This edition first published 2005

British Library Cataloguing-in-Publication Data
A catalogue record for this book is available from the British Library.

Library of Congress Cataloging-in-Publication Data
McNamara, Sarah, 1972–
   Helping young people to beat stress
      p.cm
   Includes index.
ISBN 0-8264-8755-6
1. Stress in adolescence. 2. Stress management for teenagers. 3. Life skills.
I. Title.
   BF 724. 3. 586M38 2005
   155. 518—dc22   2005049727

ISBN 0-8264-8755-6 (paperback)

Designed and typeset by Ben Cracknell Studios
Printed and bound in Great Britain by MPG Books Ltd, Bodmin, Cornwall

Contents

Acknowledgements   xi

Introduction   xvii

Practical Suggestions on How to Help Young
People to Cope more Effectively with Stress   1

CHAPTER **1**   Talking to young people about stress and
                  coping   3

**Issues to consider before starting your discussion
on stress**   3
  Setting the right tone   3
  Allowing young people to set the agenda   3
  Role shifting   4
  Confidentiality   4
  Giving the ideas a chance   5
  Follow-through   5
  Why learn more about stress?   5
  Breathing and stretching   5
  Engaging young men and women   6
  Engaging younger and older adolescents   6
  Engaging adolescents from different backgrounds   7

Sources of stress   7

The stress process   8
  Stress is part of life   8
  Internal stresses   8
  Outside stresses   8

Resources 9

The balance 9

What is stress? 10

Identity and appraisal 10

Change can be stressful 11

Positive stress 12

Daily hassles 12

Stress-related symptoms 12
Recognizing stress 12

Why do we respond in this way to stress? 15
The 'fight or flight' response 15
Stress and performance 15

CHAPTER **2**   Mental strategies for coping with stress 18

Learning to control our thoughts 19

Recognizing stress 19

'Here's one I prepared earlier' – predicting stress and being prepared 20
Learning how to plan ahead 21

Preparing for regular events 22
Dealing with stressful events 22

Keeping things in perspective 23

Replacing the negative with the positive 24

Thought stopping 26

Steps for tackling stressful thoughts 27
Examples of stressful thoughts 28

Coping skills training 29
Making a stressful events hierarchy 30
Using relaxation with the hierarchy 31
Learning to relax 32
Stress-coping thoughts 32

Problem-solving skills 34

Problem-solving as a technique 34
Stage 1. What's the problem? 34
Stage 2. Brainstorm 35
Stage 3. Give it a go! 36

The laughing cure! 37

Coping 37
A summary of stress management 38

CHAPTER **3**   Physical ways of coping with stress 41

Nutrition and eating habits 42
Healthy eating 42
Alcohol 43
Fat 45
How to reduce fat in the diet 46
Dieting and eating disorders 46

Weight and body shape 47
Does being slim bring happiness? 48
Are slim girls more attractive? 48
Our relationship with food 48
The effects of dieting 49
The best way to lose weight 49
When eating becomes a problem 49

Exercise 50
What is exercise? 50
Why exercise? 50
Why is exercise good for you? 51
Why not exercise? 52
Making exercise a part of life 52

Sleep 52
Improving sleep quality 53

Learning how to relax 54
Why should young people learn how to relax? 54

Breathing 55
Chest breathing 56
Abdominal breathing 56

Pre-menstrual syndrome 57
Coping with PMS 58

CHAPTER **4**   Study skills and time management   61

Talking to young people about studying   62

Study skills   62
   Making it easy   63
      1 Where they study   63
      2 How they study   63
      3 Why they study   64
   Making it enjoyable   64
      Body clocks   64
      Taking breaks   64
      A change is as good as a rest   64
   Finishing the study period   64
      A tidy desk is a tidy mind   64
      Use a carrot!   65
      Make it social   65
      Spread the word   65

Health and studying   65
   Body clocks and sleep   65
   Physical activity   66

Nutrition   66
   Blood sugar   66
   Caffeine   67
   Alcohol   67
   Television and music   68
   Organizing the study area   68
   Reading material   68
   Taking notes   68

Exams   69
   Prioritize   69
   Mock exams   69
   Designing a study timetable   69

Exam stress   70
   Coming up to an exam   70

Stress and worry   70
   Keep it in perspective   70

Time management   71

Exercise on time management   72
   How to manage time well   72

CHAPTER **5**   Interpersonal and communication skills   74

Relationships   76
Think about it   77
Take responsibility   77
Watch how others change   78
Solitude   78

Communication skills   79

Assertiveness   79
What is assertiveness?   79
Why be assertive?   80

Negotiation skills   80

Listen!   82

Social support   83

Bullying   83
Why intervene?   84
When to intervene   85
How to intervene   85

CHAPTER **6**   Treating yourself right   89

Treats   89

Boosting self-confidence   90
Low self-confidence   91
Confidence is complicated   91
Seeing is deceiving   92
Practice makes perfect   92
Confidence in five easy steps?   92
1   If at first …   92
2   Talk the talk and walk the walk   92
3   Learn and move on!   92
4   Don't beat yourself up!   93
5   Be nice to yourself   93

Boosting self-esteem   93
Be the devil's advocate   93
If you're the hardest judge that you could get –
tell yourself to get real!   93
All you can do is your best   94
Nurture company that nurtures   94

Unhappiness and depression 95
  What can young people do? 97
    Talk about it 97
    Use their support systems 98
  Ways of alleviating depression 98
  Thoughts of harming themselves 99

How to help prevent depression 100

Worry and anxiety 101
  What worrying achieves 101
  How to get rid of worries 102
    Worries are usually false predictions 103

CHAPTER **7**   Discussion and conclusion 105

Introduction 105

The aim of the book 105

Programme implementation 106

The socioeconomic dimension to research 109
  Overview of stress management for young people 110

References 115

Acknowledgements

I would like to thank the following people for their help and support in compiling this book. First, I would like to thank Continuum for their decision to publish and in particular Anthony Haynes, who provided essential advice, encouragement and guidance. Second, I would like to thank those who kindly agreed to review early drafts of the book and whose suggestions proved invaluable. These include Paula Mayock, Lucette McNamara, Veronica O'Doherty, Katie Baird and Molly Byrne. I would particularly like to thank Veronica for her persistent interest in the book's development. I am also grateful to the EU Training and Mobility of Researchers Fund and the Economic and Social Research Council for funding the initial research upon which the book is based. Finally, I would like to thank Michael Plumb for his support and love.

Introduction

In recent years there have been major increases in stress-related disorders in young people, including suicides, substance abuse, depression, anxiety and eating disorders.

Since the publication of *Stress in Young People: What's New and What Can We Do?* in 2000 the issue of teenage stress has become more prominent in the media, in our schools and in public awareness. A growing awareness of behavioural difficulties experienced by our young people has captured the public's imagination evidenced by a large number of television documentaries. These profile behavioural experts promising to turn teens around in relatively short time periods through behaviour management techniques. While there is some merit in these techniques, they often fail to address deeper issues such as the young person's ability to regulate their own emotions as well as their sense of inadequacy and helplessness in the face of frustrating and disempowering situations.

Perhaps the most significant development to have taken place since the first publication of this book has been the introduction of Anti-Social Behaviour Orders (ASBOs) in the UK (and soon to be introduced in Ireland). These represent an attempt to curtail anti-social behaviour particularly in young people by introducing a new layer into the criminal justice system which can target youths identified as causing trouble in local communities. This has been seen by many if not all childcare professionals as a reactionary and retrograde measure. While appearing on the surface to be a sensible strategy it is likely to alienate young people further and penalize them without looking at their real skill deficits, low self-worth and feelings of hopelessness and powerlessness.

Rising levels of classroom disruption have also been highlighted in the media, and politicians have been quick to react with suggestions of more expedient expulsions and disciplinary measures. Again, while these measures may be required, we need to look at why children are finding it so hard to sit for long periods of time in the classroom. The erosion of physical exercise from the curriculum is likely to be one factor. The failure to incorporate study skills into the curriculum may be another reason. Many students report that they lack the most basic skills in attending to one subject for more than a short period of time. We need to invest in teaching these basic building blocks to education if we are to proceed any further in educating our young people.

Increasing rates of obesity have also received a good deal of attention within public discourse. This issue is likely to have been affected by changing social landscapes which make walking and cycling more difficult, parent fears with regard to child safety and changing legislation around physical activities within schools. It also however highlights a growing use of maladaptive coping strategies and unhealthy lifestyle choices. Food may in this context be seen as a comforter in the absence of other more constructive ways to bring about a sense of calm and satisfaction.

Figures of youth suicidal ideation and attempts, levels of depression and anxiety, failure to reach societal expectations on educational attainment scores and over-sexualized behaviour all continue to show steady increases.

Since writing *Stress in Young People*, I have completed a professional diploma in clinical psychology. Two years of working with children, families and adults with mental health difficulties has served only to consolidate my belief in the importance of early education in teaching life skills and raising awareness about the key building blocks of good mental health. The pack,[1] which was published in parallel to the book, has been introduced to the Social, Personal and Health Education programmes in several countries demonstrating again the need for resources for professionals working in this area.

This book is for those who witness young people trying to come to terms with normal developmental tasks and transitions. It is also for those who are concerned with particular difficulties with which the young people in their lives are struggling. It offers evidence-based, practical, accessible guidelines to advise and empower youths to make the best decisions for themselves. At the end of the day, each person makes his or her own choices and we as adults must aim to provide as much support, information, and guidance as possible. Above all it is my belief that providing a safe, non-threatening, and open forum in which to discuss real issues with honesty is the first step in helping young people to begin to navigate this increasingly stressful life period.

The first edition of this book included a comprehensive account of the research and literature on adolescent stress. While many found this useful, the majority of those who provided feedback stated that it was in fact the latter half of the book that proved most useful. This section is reproduced here for use by parents, teachers, mental health professionals, social workers, youth workers or anyone who wishes to talk to teenagers about improving their coping skills. It is hoped that providing this practical input in a stand-alone text will make these suggestions more accessible to those at the 'frontline' who are often so badly in need of such resources. This book aims to act as a sound starting point for the types of discussions that are so essential. Readers are referred to the original text for an account of the three years of research conducted at Oxford University and comprehensive literature review that underlines all the advice contained in this book.

In summary, while views may differ on why our young people are failing to cope in increasing numbers with making the successful transition to adulthood, there remains consensus that increasing their psychological and social resources while doing so is our primary responsibility as a society that values youth. This book represents a useful resource to begin talking with teenagers in a way that will encourage them to express themselves in a safe way and learn essential coping skills to deal with the stresses of contemporary society.

Chapter 1 will help practitioners introduce young people to the area of stress and the different factors involved. Chapters 2 and 3 provide information on mental and physical ways of coping with stress. Mental ways include useful advice on how to keep things in perspective and how to keep stress levels low, as well as problem-solving and coping skills. Physical techniques of coping with stress include looking after sleep, exercise, nutrition and relaxation patterns as well as cutting down on alcohol use. Chapter 4 is devoted to study skills and time manage-ment, as many students in their exam years (and other years) find this difficult to deal with. It includes suggestions to help students to study more easily and efficiently.

The stress which arises from relationships can be the most difficult form to deal with for some people, and so ideas and issues for discussion on how to get the most out of our relationships, communication, assertiveness and negotiation skills are discussed in Chapter 5. Finally, none of these techniques will work without the self-esteem and self-confidence to carry them through, and Chapter 6 discusses ways in which young people can learn to treat themselves with respect and compassion to get the most out of their lives. A section on coping with depression and anxiety has also been included, as these may be a cause of stress in our lives or the direct consequence of our difficulties in dealing with stress. Chapter 7 discusses the meanings of the findings outlined in the book and their implications. It explains why tackling stress in young people has become so important, and why we must invest in primary prevention methods if we are to help young people to cope in the increasingly demanding world in which they live.

Notes

1 *Stress Management Programme for Secondary School Students* (2001). RoutledgeFalmer. London and New York.

Practical Suggestions on How to Help Young People to Cope more Effectively with Stress

This book provides advice, information and techniques on mental and physical ways of coping with stress, study skills and time management, communication skills, and coping with depression and anxiety. It begins by suggesting how to frame initial conversations with young people on the meaning of stress and recognizing stress.

CHAPTER 1

Talking to young people about stress and coping

The aim of Chapter 1 is to help young people identify the source of stress in their lives and the impact this has on their thoughts, feelings, health and behaviour. Having done this, you can move on to mental and physical ways of coping with stress.

The chapter aims to help you to introduce the area of stress and to get young people thinking and talking about the sources and symptoms of stress in their own lives. It will help you to discuss what they mean when they say they are stressed, how they respond when they feel stressed, when a challenging situation leads to poor coping and why they respond in this way. It discusses the benefits of learning to cope more effectively with stress, and examines the relationship between stress and performance.

Issues to consider before starting your discussion on stress

Setting the right tone

The aim of this book is to provide a guide for preventing the manifestation of stress-related symptoms in adolescents. Therefore, since these discussions are being held in a purely preventive, mental and physical health-promoting context, the tone should be one of relaxation and exploration. Young people should be encouraged to relax, to be themselves and to see this as 'time out' to explore and develop in a non-judgemental and caring environment.

Allowing young people to set the agenda

When talking to young people about stress, it is often helpful to ask them their opinion before seeking to inform them. This encourages the young person to explore issues and look back at their own experiences. It also shows young people that their views and experiences are just as important as what you have to say. Asking them to think about the issues first is also important so as not to bias the discussion, and to allow topics and issues to emerge which may not otherwise have been discussed.

As with adults, when a young person initiates a discussion it may be difficult to ascertain the root causes behind this desire to talk. Giving them the space to raise issues, asking them for their opinion, and giving them a chance to reflect on these questions before sitting down to talk properly will establish democracy within the conversation and will help to facilitate a respectful attitude from both parties. Young people are keenly aware of being 'talked down to' or 'talked at', and while this book seeks to equip you to deal with questions and help you to guide the young person, this should always be done in a consultative way with ears open at all times. These discussions should obviously be conducted with the utmost sensitivity.

Role shifting
If you are a teacher, it is worth remembering that these conversations involve a shifting of roles both for you and the young person. They require a different type of cooperation. They may require you, as the interventionist, and the young person to adapt to the new situation, particularly if they are taking place in a formal setting, such as a school. It may be worthwhile discussing this with the participants. There are no longer any right or wrong answers, and the aim of the conversation is to explore issues and experiment with new ways of looking at things.

Confidentiality
It is of fundamental importance that the issue of confidentiality is discussed with the young person. It is usually recommended that you make it clear to the young person at the outset the information which will remain confidential at all times, and the information which you may be obliged to share with appropriate others. Mandatory reporting mechanisms vary from country to country and it is important to know the law in relation to your own position. In the case of the young person disclosing that they have been the victim of sexual abuse, you may wish to inform them from the outset that you may wish to pass this information on to the relevant services. However, you can assure the young person that the decision will be made in consultation with them.

If you are conducting these discussions in a group format it is equally important that a clear discussion on confidentiality is held before the group is asked to disclose anything of a personal nature. Group members may be asked to draw up and sign a contract of confidentiality which will be of benefit to all of them in that their disclosures will be secure. The participants in the group should be encouraged not to discuss issues or incidents raised which they feel might be sensitive for other students.

Giving the ideas a chance

Having discussed confidentiality, the young people should be encouraged to be honest and open in discussions or at least to make an effort to be honest with themselves in their private reflections. This latter point is not as easy as it seems for anyone, teenagers notwithstanding.

Follow-through

You might suggest that any students or participants who wish to discuss any matters that have arisen as a result of these discussions can approach you or the school counsellor in private. Psychological back-up should be in place in conjunction with the course, with the school's permission.

Why learn more about stress?

When talking to young people about stress, it is useful to be in a position to point out the benefits of coping with stress. You can ask them to try to think of these first. Why would they want to learn more coping skills? Perhaps they feel that learning stress management or coping skills is boring, uncool or not relevant to them. You can point out that once they have learned more coping skills they will have more energy, study better and be able to relax more easily, their relationships should improve, they will have fewer headaches, better quality of sleep, feel more in control, experience improved health and probably enjoy life more.

Breathing and stretching

A good introduction to breathing and stretching exercises is provided by Whelan (1993). At the risk of being thought eccentric or a hippy from a bygone age, it is hugely helpful if you succeed in doing these exercises with the young person prior to and after any discussions on stress and coping. It will break down barriers, make them feel more relaxed, help them to realize this is 'time-out' and allow them to feel that they don't have to be in control of what they say and do, but rather can be open, relaxed and honest. It will also help them to experience the relaxing effects these exercises can have.

Engaging young men and women

With young women often tending to focus more on interpersonal and emotional stress, relationships with peers and the opposite sex are frequently cited as sources of stress. It is often more difficult to discuss stress with male students, as they are more reticent about raising these issues and can act as if nothing were wrong. These observations are consistent with the results of much research whereby males report less psychological distress. Despite the difficulties, it is crucial that we continue our efforts to engage young males by persuading them to discuss issues that are a cause of concern for them.

However, although young men sometimes look bored or act in a derisive way, it is worth holding conversations they can listen to, even if they choose not to participate. They may be behaving in a macho way while actually absorbing a good deal of the information. They often respond to very practical advice, problem-solving and humour.

Try asking them whether the issues under discussion prevent them from achieving what they want from life. If they are feeling tired, under pressure, depressed, lonely, inadequate, unable to cope, or angry without being able to express this, they are less likely to fulfil their potential and lead happy, healthy lives. Challenge them to be brave enough to give these ideas a chance. You could try experimenting with single-sex or mixed-sex discussion groups to see whether this impedes or aids the ease with which topics are discussed. Provide them with real-life experiments if they are cynical about suggestions. Assure them that young men often feel overwhelmed by the future.

Engaging younger and older adolescents

Younger adolescents are often seen to be coping with many developmental and pubertal processes and are more prone to peer conflicts and bullying. They often enjoy role-playing, games and visual representations of the ideas you are trying to communicate. Look out for cartoons or funny advertisements. Younger adolescents are often, however, very good at taking part in discussions around different issues.

Older adolescents tend to experience a higher number of conflicts with parents, and become increasingly concerned with final exams and college/employment opportunities. They may have responsibilities which include looking after younger siblings or a part-time job. Older adolescents often appreciate more mature approaches and may feel patronized by game-playing. It is important to allow them ownership of the group, to use humour and levity to oil the wheels, to be sensitive to issues which are difficult for them, and to avoid appearing over-earnest, as this can be perceived as naivety. Older students often appreciate discussions about forthcoming events. They are curious and anxious about leaving school and the challenges that lie ahead.

Engaging adolescents from different backgrounds
Sources of stress may vary depending on socioeconomic status. Financial worries may be more salient in schools in less advantaged areas, together with the vicarious stress at seeing parents unsuccessfully attempt to find employment. Pressure on students to take drugs and their side-effects can also be a source of stress. Students may witness different coping styles at home. Some research suggests that students from disadvantaged backgrounds may be less used to using problem-focused coping styles.

Students in more advantaged areas are more likely to mention exam stress and parental and internal pressure to achieve as sources of stress. Loneliness and bullying are also huge problems in boarding-schools.

Sources of stress
The following questions will help you to begin your discussion on stress and coping. If you are conducting this discussion with a large group, students should be divided into groups of four with perhaps one person allocated to feeding back the answers. Encourage them to generate answers which are meaningful and real to them, not necessarily the ones you would expect or the ones that appear in this book. In summary, before moving on to defining stress and its effects, it is recommended that young people be asked about the following.

SOURCES OF STRESS

- To generate the sources of stress in their own lives, past and present.
- To compile a list of things which have made them stressed, both in general and specific terms.
- Are the big events or the little things that happen more frequently more stressful?
- What kinds of hassles do they experience on a daily basis?
- Is stress easier when it is predictable or unexpected?
- Can stress be a positive thing?
- Can stress come from within you, as a person, as well from the outside?

The stress process
Stress is part of life

If you have been conducting this conversation in a group setting, it will become clear to the young people that everyone has experienced stress at some time, and it is normal for people to feel that they are losing control and under pressure from time to time. It is often reassuring for young people to learn that they are not alone in experiencing stress or pressure, indeed that stress is an ordinary part of life. You could even say that if you never felt stressed in your life it might mean that there was nothing in your life of value or importance to you. This means that by feeling unhappy about things like their relationships or workload, people feel a certain degree of commitment to these aspects of their lives.

The fact is that stress in young people is so common that many people are now arguing that all teenagers should be given the opportunity to learn about stress and coping at school as part of their normal curriculum. Once you have established that everyone undergoes stress from time to time, you can then proceed to unravel what this means and where this stress comes from.

Internal stresses

It is likely that when you asked for sources of stress, these consisted of external or outside stresses, like being given too much homework, being nagged by parents or being picked on by others at school. However, one of the most important lessons for young people to learn is that stress can come not only from outside but also from inside themselves. This type of stress includes their own way of looking at life and the things that happen to them and other people, their attitude to stress, coping and relaxation, and their wants, needs and feelings.

Outside stresses

Outside stresses include the pressures or burdens young people may feel they are carrying. Sources of stress that come from inside are often harder to think of for both adults and young people. Wanting to do well in school, to succeed, to be liked and to make other people happy all put pressure on the young person.

Sources of stress for young people may include carrying out necessary developmental tasks, undergoing major pubertal changes, making transitions, dealing with difficult family and peer relationships, family conflicts, academic difficulties, coping with the school environment, fear of failing exams, dealing with emerging sexuality, coping with parental separation, introduction of step-parents or parental boy/girlfriends, bullying, having nothing to do, feeling left out of a group, feeling anxious about after-school prospects, experiencing poverty or racial prejudice, parental pressure, having negative feelings about one's appearance or personal health, financial worries, losing the motivation to work, too many school and home obligations, illness or death in people they know, lacking confidence, and relationships ending.

In addition, when we get little exercise and our diet is poor, this can place stress on our bodies which may make us less able to cope and enjoy life to the full. It is normal for young people (and adults) to acknowledge only the social stresses in life. It is important to realize the contribution that the environment and physiology also make to our perceived stress levels. Once we become aware of these, we can learn to reduce them or their impact on us.

Resources

Just as stress can come from the inside as well as the outside, so too can the solutions. We often talk about two types of resources which we have to deal with stress. These are personal resources and external resources or sources of support.

You can try asking young people to think of the personal resources they have to deal with stress. Examples of resources from outside oneself include support from friends and family. Young people in their mid- to late teens are likely to ask for advice from friends as often as from family or other adults. Inside resources also come from the way the young person sees the stressful situation. This includes believing they can handle stress, the way they view themselves as a person, the way they respond to or anticipate change, religious beliefs, self-esteem, self-confidence, sense of humour and health.

The balance

What one person finds stressful, another may find an exciting challenge. Sometimes internal sources of stress combine with external sources to produce too much stress. When this happens, we can reduce the stress by (1) reducing the external stress, (2) reducing internal stress (for example, by changing attitudes), or (3) changing both. When we appraise a situation as demanding or frustrating, it causes a mental, emotional, physical and behavioural response. The strength and duration of this response is highly variable. If young people perceive the demands on them as too many and they feel they have inadequate resources, they will feel stressed and unable to cope. In other words, stress can be seen as a perception of demands as greater than resources.

You can help the young person to visualize this process by imagining demands on one side and resources on the other, like weighing scales.

What is stress?

It is always worth exploring what we mean by stress, as this is so fundamental to the way we go on to deal with it. Ask young people to define stress. Make sure you give them enough time to think their answer through. Perhaps you could ask them whether they think stress is what happens in them, the way they feel or whether it is both of these things.

These are the three most common ways of looking at stress. Perhaps stress is all three things at different times, but usually stress is both what is happening in your life and the personal attributes and social resources you bring to the situation. This can be both an exhilarating and a scary idea to take on board, as it means that we have more control over the situation than we might otherwise have thought. However, it is worth bearing in mind that young people have less control over their environments than adults and so they should balance this sense of control with an understanding that it is sometimes up to them to adjust to their situation as they may not always be able to change it. This book should help to distinguish between these different types of situations. Teaching young people that they can control how they perceive a situation does not mean that they must adjust to situations as they are. It means that they can generate more solutions. This can often involve the help of others.

Identity and appraisal

> Don't laugh at a youth for his affectations; he is only
> trying on one face after another to find his own.
> Logan Pearsall Smith.

It follows that the way young people interpret and define their experiences and what they see as the likely consequences will either relax and reassure them or make them feel stressed. If the young person interprets irritability from their parents as a sign of rejection it is likely to make them feel anxious. If they interpret the same thing as their parent feeling tired or just thinking about their own problems it will not be as worrying. Young people are often under the impression that they are the focus of other people's thoughts or concerns. This is because they are going through an important process of shaping and forming a new identity for themselves and they are heavily concerned with all aspects of this identity. They sometimes feel that others are equally concerned. It is very interesting to discuss this with groups of young people or to do role-plays which demonstrate that everyone has their own concerns.

Helping young people to understand that their interpretation of events does not always equate with reality is advice of enormous importance. Try asking them to recall events which you may have witnessed and see if you agree on all or any points. Ask them to discuss their perceptions of events honestly with their peers to see how frequently the same events are perceived differently by different people. Once they understand the role that their psychology plays, they can begin to learn coping skills that will stay with them for life.

Change can be stressful

Stress is a natural part of life. All changes which require adaptation, even when they are positive changes, can cause some stress as the young person tries to navigate a way through uncharted waters and to adapt to the new demands made by the change. Moving to a nicer house, changing to a new school class or starting a new relationship, though exciting, will all require adjustment and new things to cope with. This draws on our energy reserves and can even make us vulnerable to illness, as our resistance is lowered. This is particularly true when changes happen together or in quick succession. In many ways, adolescence is a time when both negative and positive extremes of emotion are experienced. This is one of the joys of being a teenager. In other words, whether the stress they experience is the result of major life changes such as experiencing their parents separating or moving house, or the buildup of smaller daily worries, it is how the young person responds and copes with these experiences that is important in determining the impact on their lives.

As already mentioned, teenagers are often naturally adept at staggering changes so that they don't have to deal with them all at once. This, however, is not always possible. When two or more changes occur at once, the strain on the young person may prove more difficult to cope with than if the changes had unfolded one by one. The onset of puberty may coincide, for instance, with the transition from primary to secondary school, or moving home may coincide with the young person's first relationship with a member of the opposite sex. These and other combinations can sometimes be difficult for the young person to get through. Support from those around them will help.

Unexpected events in life and situations which we have no control over are often particularly stressful. What we find stressful depends on personality, attitude, health, the circumstances surrounding the event, social support and the way our body reacts.

Positive stress

Earlier, it was suggested that you ask the young person for examples of positive stress. Although it often takes longer to think of these, remembering times when we were adrenalized is useful, as it can help us to realize what life would be like if we did not react and respond strongly to its challenges. These can be exciting and important learning experiences for us that eventuate in personal achievements we can be proud of. These include exams which, although not always seen as positive stress, can result in a real sense of reward and achievement if we are helped to cope with preparing for them. Other examples are participating in sports and falling in love.

Daily hassles

As mentioned above, daily hassles may include forgetting homework, being late, interruptions, distractions and minor conflicts. If we realize that these hassles have made us feel strained, we are less likely to lose our awareness. This can make us take it out on others and blame the wrong things for our stress.

To help them understand the centrality of appraisal and changing vulnerability, try asking young people to think of a situation when:

1 they reacted strongly to a minor hassle
2 they were calm when something major happened.

This usually helps us to realize that when we are feeling strong and in control, when things are well spaced out and we appraise them as unthreatening, we do not respond with a stress response. Sometimes we get through situations without problems and it is only later that we feel drained and tired from our coping efforts.

Stress-related symptoms

Try asking the following questions to help young people to recognize their own reactions to stress.

RECOGNIZING STRESS

- How does it feel when they're stressed?
- How would they and others know they're stressed?

- What sorts of thoughts do they have?
- How does it affect their behaviour?
- How do they relate to others at these times?
- How do other people behave towards them?
- How would they recognize stress in themselves?
- How would they recognize it in others?
- Do they know anyone who is stressed?

The aim of this section is to help young people to recognize their own symptoms of stress. This is an essential first step to coping with stress. It requires an understanding and awareness of our own well-being. Once you have helped them to recognize these symptoms, you can move on to providing them with the skills they need to alleviate or eliminate many of them.

Everyone reacts differently to increasing levels of stress. Some people become cranky while others become passive and withdrawn. Sometimes it can be difficult for adults to recognize symptoms of stress in young people or to distinguish them from mild forms of depression. This is because the symptoms of depression and stress can differ between adults and adolescents. When adolescents are feeling depressed they often appear moody, irritable and intolerant. Adults are more likely to feel numb, sad or cry a lot.

It is important for young people to be familiar with their own signs and symptoms, as this will help them to cope better with stressful situations. It is often useful to ask them to think about times in the past when they felt under pressure. If they can remember these times, they can then try to recall the symptoms they experienced. When they learn to recognize these symptoms early on they can take action before the stress gets out of hand. The following are common symptoms of stress. Ask the young people to think about which ways stress affects them. Does it depend on the situation? What types of situation affect them in these ways?

Ask the young people to think of situations when they have experienced any of these symptoms. It is important to reassure them that these things can happen more or less often when just dealing with everyday ups and downs. They may also have symptoms which are not listed here.

RECOGNIZING STRESS

Mental symptoms

They may find themselves suffering poor concentration, having difficulty remembering things, being in a hurry all the time, acting indecisively, having no confidence, over-reacting to things, feeling really tired, feeling confused, making mistakes, always putting things off, not being able to plan far ahead, always imagining the worst, worrying rather than trying to solve problems, and becoming stubborn and controlling.

Physical symptoms

They may experience muscular pains, tension headaches, aching neck, shoulders and back, stomach pains, feeling sick, choking feeling in throat, twitch in eye or lips, shakiness, clenched teeth or fists, raised heartbeat, palpitations, sweating palms, poor circulation, dry mouth, frequent urination, dizzy spells, irregular breathing, diarrhoea or constipation and allergies, asthma or skin problems becoming worse.

Emotional symptoms

They may feel irritable, aggressive, withdrawn, unable to relate as normal, lowered self-esteem, moody, cynical, guilty, anxious or feelings of panic, depressed, oversensitive to criticism, edgy, angry, hopeless, worried, miserable, feel like crying and have irrational fears.

Behavioural symptoms

They may notice that they are worse at managing time and at organizing themselves, rushing around without getting much done, sleeping or eating a lot more or less than usual, doing things in a hurry, losing touch with friends, blaming others for the problem, taking it out on others, needing a drink, turning to drugs, over-reacting, fidgeting, smoking and drinking more, behaving obsessively, or missing school a lot.

Why do we respond in this way to stress?

The 'fight-or-flight' response

Much of the way that our body responds to stress can be attributed to the fact that we have inherited a way of responding to stress through evolution called the 'fight-or-flight' response. These reactions are there to help us to cope with the threat. If we do something and the conflict is resolved, the body returns to its original state. However, if no relief comes the body may remain physically strained, which can result in long-term damage to our health. It is meant to be a temporary reaction and so cannot be maintained. When we feel threatened we release a stress hormone called cortisol. This makes us think quickly (but not very well), forget things, feel irritable and angry, and behave aggressively.

We may become vulnerable to illness after periods of stress. This is because our immune system cannot fight infection so well at these times. When we appraise situations as threatening, our body actually stops making natural killer cells and antibodies which fight against invading foreign cells.

Stress and performance

The young people you are talking to may feel that stress helps them to perform well at school or in their job. Although some stress is healthy and makes us feel challenged, young people should note the results of many studies which suggest that there is an optimum level of stress at which we feel alert and challenged. We perform well when we appraise situations as a challenge and are not confronted with overwhelming levels of stress. Having no stress can lead to us doing nothing, feeling bored and lacking energy. Too much stress will eventually burn us out and lead to us feeling totally exhausted. If maximum stress is given ten points and minimal stress is given one point, they should aim to stick to a level of around five or six points.

Conclusion

We have learned that stress is a process which starts with stressful events and minor hassles. If we perceive these as threatening they will have short- and long-term effects on our behaviour, mood, relationships and health. The intensity and duration of these effects are in part determined by many factors including social resources, personal attributes, genetic make-up and health.

KEY POINTS

In initiating your discussions with young people about stress, the key points to remember are to:

- ensure that the discussions take place in a neutral forum
- ensure that the atmosphere is relaxed and informal
- prepare them for the change of roles – there are no right or wrong answers
- discuss confidentiality
- ensure that they know who they can talk to in private about specific issues
- allow them to set the agenda in terms of the issues which are causing stress
- discuss the benefits of learning to cope more effectively with stress
- divide large groups into smaller groups of four
- experiment with single-sex and mixed-sex groups
- help to identify specific sources of stress
- encourage a discussion on internal as well as external sources of stress (attitudes, wants and assumptions)
- explore gender, age and social factors in contributing to stress and ways of coping
- ask them to think about their resources
- explore the stress of change
- discuss the symptoms of stress
- discuss how stress affects performance.

In Chapter 2 we will be learning about ways that young people can cope effectively with stress. If you intend to discuss some of these issues with young people, it is often helpful to ask them to fill out a stress diary for one week. This means recording when they felt stressed, what the preceding event was and what thoughts and feelings followed. This can help young people to be more informed about the sorts of things in their lives that are causing them stress so you can get straight to discussing ways in which they can cope better. If they would rather not share this diary (understandably), you might suggest that they jot down a summary or some thoughts on the way that stress made them feel during the course of one week.

CHAPTER 2

Mental strategies
for coping with stress

Having identified the main sources of stress for young people, this chapter aims to help you discuss coping strategies for dealing with stress together with preventive strategies which will reduce the likelihood of feelings of strain. It is useful to initiate these discussions using stress diaries to explore the events and mental precursors to feelings of tension. If you are discussing these issues in a group setting, it is important that young people know they are not required to discuss specific events or thoughts in detail (unless they want to), but rather to think about the patterns. What you are really trying to establish is the link between events, thoughts and feelings. If you are discussing this with young people in a group setting, it is a good idea to divide the larger group into groups of four for the discussion and then ask them to report back to the group as a whole. As with all discussions around stress and coping, it is a good idea to begin and end with a breathing and stretching exercise.

In your discussion you might like to ask the young people the following questions:

- What kinds of things did they find stressful from their stress diary?
- What kinds of thoughts did they have when they were stressed?
- What kinds of feelings did they experience when they were stressed?
- Which came first, the stressful *thought* or the *feelings* of stress?
- Do they notice negative thoughts saying negative things to them again and again?
- Did they notice any patterns?

Learning to control our thoughts

As we already learned in Chapter 1, appraisal is a central component in the stress process and learning how to control the way we appraise or think about things is an important key to stress management. It does not mean that we always have to change ourselves rather than the situation. It does mean that we can generate more solutions because we have a better perspective on the event. In young people, an inability to generate alternative solutions in light of highly stressful events can have serious consequences. They can feel trapped and frustrated and often try to cope with this by themselves. Suicide has been linked to a failure to generate solutions and to seeing 'no way out'.

Learning to control your thinking is a very powerful stress management tool. It allows young people to control the way situations affect them, how and if other people affect them and gives them more power to decide how they are going to live their lives.

Recognizing stress

Recognizing the problem is the first step. Awareness is the key to learning to manage stress successfully. Young people can learn to recognize signs of stress in their body, their moods or their cognitions. Unfortunately, young people may feel conditioned to hide signs of stress from others. In doing so, they are often not acknowledging it to themselves. Many young men, in particular, may feel uncomfortable about admitting to themselves and others that they feel vulnerable, strained or unhappy.

As with adults, young people will feel more vulnerable at certain times. This is influenced, for example, by their personality, the number of life changes they have experienced which require adaptation (especially recent ones), the absence or presence of social support, their general health, their nutritional status, their physical fitness, their age, previous training in learning to cope with stress or, in the case of girls, just before or during a period.

At certain times, these factors may combine to make young people feel vulnerable. Everything they have to deal with during these times when resistance is low can seem like a major obstacle. They can feel irritable and react strongly to minor hassles. At other times, young people can display enough confidence and energy to rise to any challenge.

Being aware that they are under stress and the reasons behind this is highly important for young people. If they do not recognize that they are under pressure or have insights into what may be causing the strain, it is more difficult for them to try to address this constructively and to solve the problem. The symptoms of stress were described in

Chapter 1, so you can help young people to recognize their own individual response to stress as a first step towards taking action.

Encourage young people to get into the habit of mentally noting daily stressors and their effects. If they suffer badly from stress-related symptoms you could suggest that they keep a stress diary in which, every hour, they write down what they are doing and if they have any stress symptoms, whether physical, emotional, mental or behavioural. This has already been suggested as a way of discovering more about stress for the purposes of these discussions. However, diaries can be regularly used as a stress awareness tool.

Their stress diaries will assist young people in tracing feelings of stress to events or thoughts which they may not realize came first. For example, they may have noticed that they began to feel physically tense when playing video games or watching television. They can then retrace this physical discomfort to their thoughts and feelings. Perhaps they felt guilty about not studying. Similarly, if they felt tense talking to certain people, this will relate back to their thinking in some way. Did they feel low in confidence, angry about an event in the past or dislike aspects of the interaction?

As we have seen in Chapter 1, some stress is challenging and can improve performance, so you are not trying to teach young people to remove all stress from their lives. Having nothing to do can be stressful too. The important thing is for young people to learn their limits and to recognize signs of overloading, like fatigue and crankiness, and see these as signals for a break. Unfortunately, with the huge emphasis in contemporary society on academic achievement at an earlier age, we are often so busy telling young people to work harder that we forget that in order to be happy and productive they must be healthy and relaxed too!

'Here's one I prepared earlier' – predicting stress and being prepared

We cannot stop young people making mistakes, and these are important learning tools. However, we can help them to prepare for challenging situations. It's all about seeing things as a threat or a challenge. If they feel afraid when approaching an event, their body will respond as if they are really in a threatening situation. This usually means butterflies in their stomachs, headaches and so on. If they believe they can handle the situation they will remain relaxed, both mentally and physically. This in turn sends feedback to the brain that there is nothing to worry about and they will feel more in control again. Research has shown that the effect of stress on the individual is seriously influenced by the degree of predictability and control they feel they have over it. Visualizing the event will help them to predict their responses.

Some stressful events are predictable, such as sitting exams. Other situations can make us feel uncomfortable without knowing why. A stress diary will help young people to see patterns in stressful situations. Once they know the problem, they can plan productively how to cope with it.

It is commonly known that worrying about a forthcoming event is an energy drain and achieves little. However, proper preparation for events which we know are going to happen can be a fantastic stress management tool. For young people, these can include school tests, confrontations with peers, dates and difficult discussions about the future.

LEARNING HOW TO PLAN AHEAD

Suggest that young people think of a stressful situation they are presently dealing with or know is coming up. Then suggest that they:

- *Imagine* it in detail, particularly how they are likely to feel. Rehearse this while doing breathing and stretching exercises.

- Start *preparing* – if it is their reaction to aggressive comments which is likely to be stressful, they should prepare for ways of dealing with these comments without feeling upset. If it is not being able to answer a particular question on an exam paper, they could get extra help with that subject, talk to other students about it or try doing a bit more reading on it.

- Be familiar with *likely possibilities* and decide that they will be calm and relaxed.

- Make *contingency* plans – these will make it seem less threatening; for example, if they are asking someone along to something that they really want to go to, they should have someone else in mind who they can ask if their first choice can't make it.

- Do some *relaxation* before the situation. Going for a run or doing some breathing and stretching exercises should help.

- Plan *relaxation* time as well as a *reward* for after the stressful event.

Preparing for regular events

As with adults, for young people much of their stress will come from regular situations such as having to talk to people they don't like, being behind with homework, or witnessing conflicts. If they can learn to see these situations coming and prepare for them they will be less likely to get upset, because they will feel more in control. Again, their stress diary will be useful to help them to identify the types of stress that come up frequently or regularly. You can suggest the following as some ideas for dealing with regular stressful events.

DEALING WITH STRESSFUL EVENTS

1 *Get out* of the situation when appropriate (e.g. by not mixing with peers who make them feel uncomfortable).

2 *Prepare* (e.g. get their homework done early).

3 *Meet* the situation head-on (e.g. go and talk to a source of stress).

4 *Decide* what is best at keeping stress levels down – ask them to think about the way they normally handle a situation and if this is working for them. If not, then it is time to *re-evaluate their strategy*. For instance, if ignoring a friend every time they upset them or arguing with parents over homework results in them getting upset, perhaps they need to think of other ways of handling these situations.

Sometimes young people feel that anticipation is not necessary or natural, but for us to cope successfully we need to anticipate problems so that we can plan to take the most appropriate actions which will lead to the best outcomes for us. After we have been engaged in positive anticipation for a while, we can then re-evaluate the situation by asking the following questions: Have we been successful in achieving our *goal*? Can we *improve* our strategy? Would changing our strategy be more *beneficial*? (e.g. talking to someone directly rather than showing our annoyance by ignoring them).

When discussing these issues with young people, it is always helpful to relate them to real experiences and examples produced by the young people themselves.

Keeping things in perspective

Again, the simple three-way relationship between events, thoughts and feelings can help young people to understand that their feelings, whether they are ones of anxiety, depression or worry, have been produced by their thought processes and this is where they need to intervene in order to restore their emotional balance. This can then help them to change their objective circumstances by making them feel more in control.

When they feel upset or under pressure, young people are likely to:

- view everything in black and white

- generalize

- attach disproportionate significance to a particular aspect of an event

- think in a very extreme way

- exaggerate the consequences of the situation

- look only at the bad things

- take things personally

- blame themselves or other people in an irrational way

- jump to conclusions which are often unfounded.

This will lead to much more anxiety as, unfortunately, the body will react according to the way the mind has *interpreted* the situation, and thus stress can often continue or be made worse. This is because the mind is insisting on telling the body that we are in some kind of danger. If young people can learn to replace these extreme thoughts with more realistic and helpful ones they can learn to tone down their stress response. You can suggest that instead of using words such as 'always', 'never', 'must' and 'should', they can use 'often', 'rarely' and ' might'.

The following are common examples: 'I *never* do anything right', '*Nothing* is going right for me', '*Nothing* good is ever going to happen', 'I can *never* adapt to this' and 'There is *no one* who loves me'.

Much research has shown that those people who reinterpret a stressful situation more positively experience less intense physiological response and take less time to recover.

You can suggest an experiment: the next time the young people feel tense or stressed, they can try following their thoughts and challenge them. They can practise re-labelling the situation by trying to be more moderate and positive. If they do this, they will notice how much more quickly they return to feeling relaxed.

Replacing the negative with the positive

Man is not disturbed by events, but by the view he takes of them.
Epictetus.

Everybody has private conversations with themselves every day. We all have a critical inner voice that can hound us, making us feel strained, inadequate and low in confidence. These conversations can take the form of negative statements about ourselves. Young people in particular can experience doubts about themselves and what they can achieve. It is a vulnerable time when they compare themselves with peers and often receive criticism and conflicting messages from all around them. These internal conversations can bring self-doubt about their abilities to, for example, do well in school, cope with tense family relationships, start a career or form a relationship. It can make them come down on themselves, for example, when they tell themselves that 'I always mess things up', 'I look horrible', 'I have nothing to offer anyone', 'I don't fit in', or 'I'll never make a success of anything'.

Praise youth and it will prosper.
Irish proverb.

It is important to discuss these types of internal conversations with young people as they are constantly chipping away at their feelings of *self-worth* and emphasizing their weak points in an irrational way. Young people need to be encouraged, praised and supported. We often tend to forget that they are their own worst critics.

You can ask young people to think of things they say to themselves about themselves which may not be true. These may contain references to themselves that are so taken for granted that they are not even aware of the immediate increases in stress which follow and the resulting feelings. Unless they feel very comfortable in a group, it is unlikely they will want to share these thoughts as they relate to their most intimate images of ourselves.

They can look for clues as to what these statements to ourselves sound like. For instance, when we find ourselves over-using the word 'should'; for example, 'I should always be fun to be with or I'll lose my friends', 'I should always look confident and in control' or 'I shouldn't need any help from others'.

We are all inclined to think in an extreme way about our personal life; for example, if we don't have a partner we might feel it's the end of the world, or if people fail to ring us we feel utterly rejected. Young people can learn to be more moderate and realistic in the way they choose to interpret situations.

In summary, the way young people feel is not just about the actual events. In between the event and the feelings lie internal conversations which may be realistic or unrealistic. It is this 'self-talk' that produces the emotions. The way we think, directed and controlled by ourselves, is what creates negative feelings of anxiety, hostility and unhappiness.

A typical example of how this can affect young people is the negative self-talk which follows when they feel they have been excluded by their peers. Learning to reinterpret people's behaviour so that their self-esteem does not suffer is important. For example, they can learn that when friends don't call, it is often to do with other circumstances than their own popularity. If we can only impress upon young people that there are several ways of seeing things, we have introduced an element of doubt into this chain that can weaken it, even if they are not totally convinced!

The emotional outcomes of irrational self-talk are anxiety, depression, anger, guilt and low self-esteem. These internal conversations represent the way we view the world. If the self-talk is accurate and in touch with reality, we function well. If it is irrational and untrue, we experience stress and emotional distress.

Albert Ellis (1984) developed a system to attack irrational ideas or beliefs and replace them with realistic statements about the world. He believed that we *do* have a choice in how we train ourselves to view the things we experience. Negative training will lead to stress, while positive training will act as an antidote in times of stress. The following are common negative self-talks and the alternative positive statements. You can give this as an exercise for young people to fill out to practise seeing things from a different perspective.[1] Here are some of the possible ways that these can be answered.

- *Negative*: I can't help it if people or events stress me out.
- *Positive:* It's my decision whether I let these things get to me.
- *Negative*: I can't control the way I feel or how long I feel this way.
- *Positive:* I can actually control how long I feel like this and how much it hurts.

- *Negative*: It runs in the family. My father was just like me.
- *Positive:* This doesn't mean I have to be. I can change this behaviour.
- *Negative*: I need everything to work out well.
- *Positive:* That's life, not everything works out. I have to learn to take the rough with the smooth.
- *Negative*: How can anyone behave like this towards me when I've been so good to them?
- *Positive:* In an ideal world things like this wouldn't happen, but there is probably a reason for this person's behaviour.
- *Negative*: This is unbearable.
- *Positive:* I have the strength to deal with this and there are others who can help me. I have to keep things in perspective.
- *Negative*: I'm no good at anything.
- *Positive:* I have to focus on what I'm good at.
- *Negative*: Things will never get better for me.
- *Positive:* I have to be positive. Things will work out.
- *Negative*: I always ruin everything.
- *Positive:* Sometimes things don't work out as planned, but it happens to everyone and I try my best.

Thought stopping

'Thought stopping' is a technique that can help people to overcome thoughts which cause stress and worry and which prevent them from being able to relax. It was originally introduced as a therapy aid for people suffering from obsessive, nagging worry and doubt, and has since been used in the treatment of depression, anxiety, phobias and panic attacks. It can help in day-to-day life.

Many young people experience recurring thoughts which cause them anxiety. Typical ones include feeling unattractive, unpopular, unintelligent or incompetent. Persistent thoughts may take the form of self-doubt; for example, feeling that they will never succeed at school, or have a relationship. They may also take the form of anxiety; for example, worrying about their parents splitting up or things not working out.

Thoughts like these can understandably cause a lot of stress. Thought stopping is a simple but surprisingly effective technique. First of all young people must know the sorts of thoughts they are likely to have and then to switch off and empty their mind. They can either simply say 'STOP' to themselves, or they can get into the habit of replacing these thoughts with reassuring and more constructive, rational statements such as 'I won't fail if I work a little harder, it'll be fine'. These are the sorts of reassurances that young people seek from others, but unfortunately adults and friends may not know on which points they need reassurance. While reassurance from others is important, it is also important to be able to treat oneself with the compassion and support we seek from others.

If you are conducting a conversation with young people about recurring thoughts, you can try asking them to 'take a reality check' on these thoughts they may have learned to live with by asking themselves the questions in the box on pp. 28–9. The process of challenging their rationale is in itself a useful one. For instance, adolescents who harm themselves have often become so used to telling themselves that they are useless, unattractive or unloved that they never challenge these thoughts. While this method of stress management cannot uproot the possible negative messages which young people have absorbed, it can alleviate the symptoms and protect young people from suffering unduly. Issues around self-esteem are discussed in Chapter 6.

Ask them to think of a negative thought about themselves which they have often. Then ask them to think about the following questions. If they feel comfortable enough they could discuss them with you or a friend: Does the thought seem rational or irrational? Is it useful or useless in helping them get on in life? Do they find it difficult or easy to stop thinking these thoughts? Where might these thoughts have come from?

This type of coping skill undoubtedly requires discipline, but it is something that we can train ourselves to do. Ask the young person to choose one recurring thought and decide that it is unrealistic, unnecessary and an obstacle to their happiness.

Ironically, thoughts like these can cause so much anxiety that they stop people from doing what they need to do to ensure that they don't come true! Many teachers and parents have witnessed this in relation to teenagers who worry so much about their exams that it impedes their ability to study effectively. Thought stopping involves concentrating on the unwanted thoughts and, after a short time, suddenly stopping and emptying your mind.

Steps for tackling stressful thoughts

You can ask the young people to try the following exercise which involves identifying persistent stress-producing thoughts and rating them on a scale of one to five for the discomfort (how painful and intrusive they are to them, regardless of how big or small they would appear to others) and interference they cause. Any thought with a rating of over three for discomfort and over two for interference may warrant thought-stopping procedures.

The following is a list of stressful thoughts experienced by most people from time to time. If they begin to cause the young person undue distress as they cannot take their mind off them and they begin to intrude on their lives, they may want to try thought stopping as a way of reducing the stress that they cause. Some worries are there for a reason, and there are obviously things that young people are concerned about which might happen. In this case young people should obviously be encouraged to take appropriate action. Deciding what recurrent thoughts are necessary and what are just energy drains that make us feel anxious is discussed further in Chapter 6.

EXAMPLES OF STRESSFUL THOUGHTS

Do they find themselves:

- worrying about their physical or mental health?

- feeling guilty all the time?

- worrying all the time about having said the wrong thing?

- having unpleasant or frightening thoughts or words going over and over in their mind?

- being troubled by certain thoughts of harming themselves or others?

- going over and over a job that's finished, thinking that they could have done it better?

- being unable to make even simple decisions?

- having constant doubts about everything?

- having an irrational fear about doing certain things?

- always thinking things will get worse?

- feeling engrossed in anger when people don't do things the way they would like?

- thinking about details all the time?

- having ongoing feelings of jealousy, or fear of being rejected?

- preoccupied with desire for things they cannot have?

- preoccupied with negative aspects of their appearance?

- thinking again and again about their failures?

- thinking a lot about things they are ashamed of?

- worrying frequently about what the opposite sex thinks of them?

- worrying constantly about failing their exams?

In summary, thought stopping involves (1) imagining the thought, (2) saying 'Stop!' every time you start saying this to yourself, (3) thinking of a positive, assertive statement that will make you feel the way you want to feel. For example, if you are nervous about asking someone out and always say to yourself 'I'm too unattractive', say instead 'I've got a lot to offer!' This procedure may sound simple, but when practised regularly with discipline it has helped many people overcome thoughts which recur and cause stress and pain.

Coping skills training[2]

Like thought stopping and changing irrational thinking, coping skills training is about replacing stress-inducing thoughts with more constructive thinking, this time using relaxation techniques. This technique is also called 'stress inoculation' and was developed by Meichenbaum (1977). Coping skills training teaches people to relax away anxiety and stress reactions. It gives us more self-control in the particular situation that we find anxiety-provoking.

As is the case with adults, some young people are better at coping in certain situations than others. Coping skills training centres around learning to relax using progressive muscle relaxation, so that when we encounter stress we find it easy to release the tension.

The first step is to construct a list of *stressful situations* and arrange the list from the least threatening to the most threatening situation. Using their imagination, young people can call up each of those situations and learn to relax away any stress they feel. They can then learn to create their own personal list of stress-coping remarks which they can say to themselves at times of stress, rather than the usual comments we say to ourselves, such as: 'I can't do this . . . I'm not good enough . . .', 'Everyone else is more on top of things than me . . .'.

Making a stressful events hierarchy
Making a list of all our current life situations which trigger anxiety is important if we are to start tackling these with coping skills training. When writing this list, young people should include any stressful event they are likely to encounter in the relatively near future (e.g. finding it hard to study, worry about exams, problems with family or friends, boy/girlfriend problems). They should get as close to twenty items on their list as possible. These can run from mild discomfort to their most dreaded experiences.

This list can be turned into a hierarchy by ranking the stressful experiences in order, from the least to the most anxiety-provoking. Each item on the list should represent an increase in stress over the last item, and the increases should be approximately equal. To do this, Wolpe (a leading researcher on coping skills) has recommended that we rate each situation as *Stressful Units of Distress* (SUDS). Being fully relaxed is zero SUDS, while the most stressful situation in their hierarchy should be rated at 100 SUDS. All the other situations are between one and 100.

There are huge individual differences in what people find stressful. Discussing this with young people can be interesting in itself and reassuring to realize that things which may be unproblematic to some cause major anxiety to others. This can help boost confidence.

EXAMPLE OF A STRESSFUL EVENTS HIERARCHY

Rank	Item	SUDS
1	Rushing to get to school on time	10
2	Parents hassling me about housework	15
3	Having to attend a class in which I don't like the teacher	20
4	Having problems settling down to homework	25
5	Bad mark in essay	30
6	Friends falling out with each other	35
7	Not being allowed to go to a club with my friends	40
8	Parents arguing in front of me	45
9	Anxious over exams	50

10	Feeling sick	55
11	Trying to make conversation with someone I fancy	60
12	Being pressured to take drugs	65
13	....	......
14	....	......
15	....	......
16	....	......
17	....	......
18	....	......
19	....	......
20	Worried about pregnancy/girlfriend pregnant	100

. . . and so on.

Using relaxation with the hierarchy

This list can be used to help learn how to relax while experiencing stress. Young people can begin with the first situation (lowest SUDS) and build a clear picture of the situation in their imagination. They can try to hold on to the image for about half a minute. They should notice the beginning of any tension in their body and any sense of anxiety. This sensation of tension should be used as a signal for deep muscle relaxation and deep breathing. Tightening in our body is like an early warning system of what later will be real emotional discomfort. It is possible to relax away this tension, even as we imagine the stressful situations.

When they have imagined a particular scene twice without feeling tense or anxious, the young people can go on to the next situation in their list. Over the next few days they can move through their entire hierarchy of stressful situations following the same steps, going from the least to the most stressful. At the end, they will have a deeper awareness of how and where tension builds in their bodies. They can learn to welcome early signs of tension as their signal to relax. Mastering the situations with the highest SUDS provides a degree of confidence that stress reduction is possible, even in the most threatening situations.

To learn this relaxation skill, each scene must be clear and realistic. This means making a real effort to conjure up all aspects of the situation including the way things sound, smell, look and feel. The more they practise, the easier it will be to feel as if they're really there.

When they begin practising relaxation this way, young people should not push beyond three or four scenes. When they're ready, usually after four or five days, they should have made it through their list. They should then feel a great deal more confident about dealing with these situations in real life.

Learning to relax

Progressive muscle relaxation is often used for this exercise. This involves lying down and focusing on one muscle at a time, starting from your toes and moving up your body. You tense each muscle for a few seconds and then relax that muscle. They can try this at home alone or with a group in school or other group setting. Suggestions for physical ways of coping with stress together with the directions for progressive relaxation are provided in Chapter 3.

Learning to breathe from your abdomen is the key to relaxation. This is called deep breathing. Suggest that students put their hands on their abdomen and breathe in so that they feel the air expanding their tummy and pushing out their hands. They should then breathe deeply and try to reach a comfortable rhythm, feeling the air push their hands. They should breathe out with a sigh, and visualize the tension flowing out of their body as they let go of each breath.

Students can practise and prepare for these situations by imagining them in detail. When they are imagining them, they will begin to notice tension in their body, their muscles will start to tense, or they will have feelings of upset, anger or anxiety. When they feel these, they will know that they need to begin relaxing their body. When this happens they need to take some deep breaths, making sure they are breathing from their stomach, and to begin by tensing up each muscle from their toes to their neck and then releasing the tension.

Stress-coping thoughts

Once they are comfortable using these relaxation skills, young people are ready to create their own repertoire of stress-coping self-statements. To understand how they work, it is useful to consider the four components of an emotional response.

1 *Event*: Their teacher gives them a lecture about not doing enough work.

2 *Physical response*: Their automatic nervous system produces symptoms such as feeling tense, their muscles get tighter. . . .

3 *Action*: They attempt to deal with the situation by apologizing or becoming defensive and getting away as quickly as possible.

4 *Thoughts*: Their appraisal of the situation, predictions and self-evaluations are what creates emotion. If at this point they say to themselves, 'I can't stand this. . . . It's too much for me. . . .', then the emotional response will be fear. If their self-statements are 'I've had enough of him/her telling me what to do all the time, God, I hate that teacher . . . ', then their emotional response is likely to be one of anger.

Their *interpretations* of the incident, how they imagine it will affect the future and what they say to themselves about their own worth are the ways they select and intensify the emotions they will feel.

Using coping skills training while going through a stressful situation, young people can begin using calming statements such as 'Relax. . . . Breathe deeply. . . . You've been through this before. . . . Stay calm. . . . He can't really affect me'.

The final stage in this technique, after they have gone through their hierarchy of stressful situations in their *imagination*, is to learn to apply coping skills to *real-life situations*. When they feel stress, they use their body tension as a cue to relax. They can also use the stress-coping thoughts they have learned to reassure, relax and congratulate themselves when the event is over.

The more attention they give to their coping statements, the quicker will come relief from physiological arousal and over-reaction. They will feel much better. Suggest that they make their own list of stress-coping thoughts and learn them, as these will be the most useful.

Young people can then prepare things they say to themselves at each stage while confronting the stressful situation. While preparing, they can tell themselves, *'there's nothing to worry about'*, *'I've done this before'*, *'I'll just start and it will get easier'*. While dealing with the situation they can tell themselves *'I can only do my best'*, *'I just need to focus'*, *'I can get help if I need it'*. If they feel anxious, they can say to themselves, *'If I feel tense, I know now how to relax'*, *'I need to breathe deeply'*, *'I can handle this'*. After the situation they need to reward their efforts and congratulate themselves for getting through it, and they can tell themselves, *'I went through it, and coped'*, *'Next time it won't be so bad'*.

Encourage them to learn some statements for each stage of coping: preparing, facing the event, feeling anxious and congratulating themselves for getting through it. They should put the list somewhere convenient, such as on their desks or in their bedrooms, and get used to seeing it regularly.

In summary, coping skills training provides rehearsal in imagination for the real-life events that young people may find distressing. They can learn to relax in the imagined scenes and are thereafter prepared to relax away tension when under fire, when facing deadlines for homework, when in an argument, when in exams and so on. Eventually, self-relaxation procedures and stress-coping thoughts become automatic in any stressful situation. Coping skills training has been shown to be effective in the reduction of general anxiety as well as exam anxiety.

Problem-solving skills[3]

A good deal of research has shown that problem-solving ability in young people represents a resiliency factor which makes them less likely to experience maladaptive outcomes both in adolescence and in adulthood. Problem-solving is a skill which can be applied in many situations and, once learned, can stay with us for life. As mentioned above, failure to acquire problem-solving skills or undervaluing the role of problem-solving has been linked to suicidal attempts in male and female teenagers.

Problem-solving as a technique

Many of us consider problem-solving to be such a simple and effective technique that we underestimate what an important stress management tool it is. We cannot assume, however, that the young people with whom we are engaged will have experienced a strong culture of problem-solving. Some parents are more inclined to react with emotion or sanction in the event of problems relating to their teenage children and so it may be that young people have yet to witness the positive benefits which effective problem-solving can bestow.

The use of problem-solving is associated with better adaptation. The important thing is to be methodical in the way we approach problems. Again, as with the other mental strategies for coping with stress, it is always helpful to ask young people to think of a real example before engaging them in this exercise.

Stage 1. What's the problem?

This is the most obvious and yet the most difficult part of the process. The problem must be clearly identified and defined. Often when we feel stressed or upset we have vague feelings of strain, sadness, irritability or fatigue. These are much harder to combat than clearly defined problems.

All the work they have done on awareness of stress and tracing these feelings back to thoughts and events will be a huge bonus to young people at this stage. However, it can still remain difficult to identify what the exact problem is. For example, a teenager might complain that he or she feels 'stressed out' because their mother's new partner is leaving the house in a mess or invading their privacy. The real problem may lie somewhere else altogether and may focus around unresolved conflicts with this new person. Perhaps there has been no attempt to include them in decisions around the new arrangement.

If young people are finding it hard to specify what their problems are, they might try speaking to someone they respect and trust and who knows them well, taking time out to allow them to gain a clearer perspective, and asking themselves questions such as do they feel worse during the day or at night, at home or school, with friends or family, working or relaxing.

Sometimes we find it difficult to be clear and honest about where difficulties lie. This may be because the problem is a deep-seated one and one that is painful to explore. Even in these cases, acknowledging the problem is the first step towards solving it. Counsellors are highly skilled in helping people move on from here.

Stage 2. Brainstorm

Generating solutions to problems is an innate skill for some, but the rest of us have to work hard at it. We can promote this skill by learning how to discuss things with different people, not shooting down solutions too early, trying to see things from different perspectives or making a list.

You could ask young people to choose one of the problems they have already identified at Stage 1, and do a brainstorming exercise to think of as many solutions as they can. They can ask a friend to help them and write down each of the possible solutions. They can use the ideas suggested by the friend as a springboard to help reactivate their own problem-solving. The important point is not to reject a solution at an early stage however stupid or way out it sounds, but to write it down and go on thinking about other possible solutions. Brainstorming is now becoming fashionable in practically every setting, not just for war strategies. Businessmen are increasingly using it to generate new ideas and escape old ways of thinking. It can be just as dynamic when used to solve our own personal problems.

In summary, this stage involves (1) defining the problem, (2) suggesting whatever solutions come to mind, (3) not censoring these regardless of how much sense they make at first, and (4) noting these ideas and continuing.

Stage 3. Give it a go!
The young people should then:

- Look through their list of solutions and *choose* which one looks the most encouraging and helpful. It may help to discuss this with someone whose opinions they value and trust.
- *Have a go*. They should then work out exactly what it would involve, and take the necessary steps.
- *Assess the outcome*. The solution they have selected may or may not work. If it works, they need to remember this so that they can do it again if they need to, or persist if it looks as if it has put them on the right track. If it doesn't work, it is even more important that they know, so that they can go back to their list of solutions and try something else. Many solutions are helpful but do not provide the complete answer. They need to know this also so that they can work out whether to persist with the chosen solution or to look for further solutions. Whatever happens, they need to evaluate it.
- *Keep going* until they feel better. Their assessment might show that they are on the right track but have not gone far enough. Problems are often not solved overnight. Some persistence is usually necessary.

PROBLEM-SOLVING: FOUR MORE THINGS TO REMEMBER

1 *Move on*. If the problem cannot be solved, move on and forget about it. There is no point wasting time 'flogging a dead horse'.

2 *One thing at a time*. Sometimes young people can feel inundated with pressures, which all seem to come at once. Effective problem-solving can often mean solving one problem at a time.

3 *You can only change yourself*. If the problem is a social one, there is a chance that, when you ask young people what needs to happen, they will recommend that someone else needs to change their behaviour. For problem-solving to be successful, young people have to rely on changes they can make in

themselves. They need to take responsibility for their role in the problem. This is discussed further in Chapter 5.

4 *Accepting is acceptable*. Sometimes they may have to accept that the best thing to do is to do nothing. Accepting a problem and deciding to cope with it is sometimes a valid solution.

The laughing cure!

As someone who has worked or intends to work with young people, you will know the difference that humour can make to our relationships with young people. If you tell a joke or a young person jokes, this can bring much needed levity and good feelings into what would otherwise be tense, uncomfortable or simply joyless situations. We all remember teachers at school whose sense of humour brought them respect and affection. Being humorous, without sarcasm, in appropriate situations when talking to young people is also a good lesson in keeping perspective.

The knowledge that laughter is the best medicine is part of folklore and, like any folk remedy, we are usually sceptical about it, unless there is scientific evidence to back the claim or we have had personal experience of its benefit. There are, however, scientifically proven benefits to having a good laugh. It releases serotonin and endorphins, which are natural tranquillizers and immediately improve our mood. In addition, when we laugh we are more likely to breathe from our bellies which helps us relax, we take in more oxygen which is invigorating, our facial expressions feed back to our brain and tell us that we are happy. Humour makes us look at things in a different, lighter and less threatening way.

Coping

Studies show that the more coping skills one has, the better, i.e. using humour, problem-solving, detaching, relationships, recreation, confrontation and so on. We often talk about approach or problem-solving coping as opposed to avoidance or emotion-based coping.

- *Approach coping* sometimes means seeing your stress as a problem and taking steps towards solving it.
- *Avoidance coping* can mean ignoring the problem or trying to find ways to distract yourself.

For young people, using approach coping is probably most helpful in situations in which they have a degree of control. Avoidance coping may help when there is nothing they can do except accept the situation or tune out.

A SUMMARY OF STRESS MANAGEMENT

In the remainder of this book many more ways of dealing with stress are discussed. In summary, in order to keep their stress levels down, young people need to:

1 Look around

Gauge the pressure – Realize how much they have on their plate at any one time. They need to include daily hassles and recent changes that required adaptation; even if the changes aren't in themselves negative, they may represent energy drains.

2 Look inwards

- They need to be familiar with their own symptoms – Do they get irritable or sad? Do they think negatively or tend to overgeneralize, do they become inactive or try to do too much?

- Are they aware of changes in themselves that might be due to a buildup in stress? They should think about the way they think, act and feel.

3 Look ahead

They should always try to think about whether the solutions they choose will help them in the long run as well as the short term.

4 Look back

Think about the patterns in their relationships or the way they have dealt with similar situations in the past and try to learn from them whether they were helpful or unhelpful, rational or irrational. Think about where these patterns might have come from.

5 Look after themselves

- Take breaks when the pressure gets too much.

- Do one thing at a time. Eat, rest, exercise and socialize without doing other things at the same time.

- Make lists to aid memory and help with planning and time management.

- Remember to BREATHE – that means watching breathing, relaxation, exercise, reducing alcohol and tea and coffee, and healthy eating.

- Learn not to procrastinate: putting off doing things makes us feel stressed, guilty and tired. Get down to it and then relax.

- Be nice to themselves. Treat themselves the way they would like others to treat them, with care and respect. Learn to lose all those undermining attitudes which bring them down.

- Make sure they relax, have fun and nurture their relationships.

CONCLUSION

To help young people improve their mental strategies for coping with stress:

1 Discuss the link between events, thoughts and feelings.

2 Encourage them to see this pattern in everyday situations.

3 Suggest they keep a stress diary.

4 Familiarize them with the symptoms of stress – emphasize the importance of recognizing stress.

5 Explain the key role of appraisal in the stress process.

6 Encourage them to be aware of the effects of sources and symptoms of stress.

7 Present advice on:

- learning how to plan ahead

- preparing for negative events

- keeping things in perspective

- thought stopping

- coping skills training

- learning how to relax

- problem-solving

- laughing

- coping.

You should suggest that people keep an exercise, sleep and diet diary for one week, as Chapter 3 discusses the effects these have on stress and coping. They could record what they eat and drink and how much exercise and sleep they get each day, and their levels of stress this and the following day.

Notes

1 See Patel, C. (1989) *The Complete Guide to Stress Management*. London: Vermillion.
2 Davis, M., Eshelman, E. and McKay, M. (1995) *The Relaxation and Stress Reduction Workbook* (4th edition). Oakland, CA: New Harbinger Publications.
3 Butler, G. and Hope, T. (1995) *The Mental Fitness Guide: Manage Your Mind*. Oxford: Oxford University Press.

CHAPTER 3

Physical ways of coping with stress

This chapter looks at physical ways in which we can help to combat stress. This includes looking after nutrition, sleep and exercise in order to keep our immune system strong and our energy levels high. We will also learn more about relaxation and premenstrual tension.

Feeling healthy and fit can prevent young people from feeling undue strain when they encounter stressful events in their lives. It may even prevent some of these events from occurring in the first place. For instance, if young people are exercising, eating and sleeping well, they may study better and so limit exam stress, they may relate better and so limit relationship stress and so on. Persistent stress can also lead to many physical complaints, including tension headaches, migraine, backache, palpitations and chest discomfort, allergies, coughs and colds, asthma, high blood pressure, angina (chest pain), anxiety, chronic fatigue, irritable bowel syndrome and ulcers.

The following questions will help you to begin your discussion with young people on areas of health which are important for stress prevention. If you have asked them to keep the diaries suggested in Chapter 2, you can use these as a basis for your discussions. These are useful in that they allow discussions to begin in an informed and realistic way based on accurate estimates of sleep, exercise and nutrition as well as how young people felt during the week.

Before beginning a discussion on physical well-being, it is a good idea to simply ask young people what they feel would enhance their physical well-being. These days, young people are provided with a good deal of information about health. If you begin by assuming they do not already have this knowledge, you risk patronising them and wasting time. If they appear to already possess a good understanding of the basic tenets, move on to how they have applied these in their own lives. Chances are you can be helpful in discussing the obstacles to applying these principles.

Nutrition and eating habits[1]

You can begin this discussion by asking young people to look at their food diaries. If they haven't kept a diary, you can have a general discussion based on the same questions.

HEALTHY EATING

- Do they feel their diet is healthy?
- How do they feel after eating certain foods?
- Do they feel energetic in general?
- Do they often feel tired?
- Do they have trouble concentrating?
- Do they skip meals?
- How much caffeine do they drink?
- How much water do they drink?
- Do they eat breakfast?

Eating well is crucial to good health, and being healthy will help young people cope better with life's stresses. It is a useful skill to recognize the foods which make us feel energetic and positive and those which can make us feel fatigued and negative. Nutrition plays a vital role in warding off headaches, sluggishness, irritability and even premenstrual syndrome. It boosts the immune system, thus keeping us healthy and able to cope.

Despite the fads which come and go, there are basic general principles to healthy eating. These are to reduce saturated fats, sugar, salt, caffeine and alcohol and to increase fibre and starches, fruit and vegetables. Diets should also contain a variety of foods, individuals should try to maintain their ideal weight, and use exercise to regulate appetite and weight.

It is also recommended that we eat calm, frequent meals and take a multi-vitamin tablet daily if we are feeling run down. Nutrition must be understood as a whole system; in other words there are no good and bad foods, only good and bad diets. Eating the odd bar of chocolate and fast food meal is only important in the way it fits into the overall diet, i.e. how regular it is and what other foods we are eating.

Starches are also referred to as complex carbohydrates and should form the main source of energy in our diet. They exert such a positive effect on mood that they have been referred to as natural tranquillizers. This is because they cause the release of serotonin which improves mood. It is recommended that the bulk of our calorific intake comes from starches. Examples include potatoes, rice, pasta, bread, porridge, breakfast cereal and muesli. Young people are often worried that these foods are fattening. However, you can reassure them by informing them that contrary to this belief they can actually keep weight down by controlling the appetite and preventing the sudden drops in blood glucose levels which cause snacking. It is best to eat wholegrain varieties – wholemeal bread or pasta, brown rice – because they contain more fibre, vitamins and minerals and are also more filling.

Protein is required for growth and repair of body tissues. Starches, fruit and vegetables should be eaten in much greater quantities than protein.

Young people should get all the *vitamins and minerals* they need from eating a well-balanced diet and particularly from fresh fruit and vegetables. However, if they are not eating well, they may feel tired and run down. In these cases, you should recommend that they take a multi-vitamin course. If they feel their diet contains insufficient nutrients, they should discuss this with their parents.

On average we require at least one litre of *water* a day. If they are eating a lot of fast food, young people may need more water as it contains a lot of salt. Those who take regular exercise will also need to drink more. It is worth telling them that many soft drinks actually dehydrate the body.

Caffeine is contained in coffee, tea, chocolate and some carbonated drinks. Because it is a stimulant, caffeine can contribute to irritability, tiredness, and sleep problems. It is often a surprise for people to work out exactly how much caffeine they actually consume. You can help young people to estimate how much their daily caffeine intake is by referring to Table 3.1 on p. 44. The recommended amount of caffeine per day is 200 mg, which is about one cup of brewed coffee.

Alcohol

Alcohol is high in calories and can therefore lead to weight gain. A gram of alcohol contains seven calories, which is nearly twice as much as sugar. In addition, alcohol reduces our body's ability to break down fat because it slows down the body's metabolism, and the liver processes the alcohol rather than burning fat.

Table 3.1 *Caffeine content in drinks*

Type of drink	Serving	Caffeine
Brewed coffee	10 oz	170–200 mg
Decaffeinated coffee	10 oz	10 mg
Instant coffee	10 oz	90–140 mg
Tea	10 oz	60–100 mg
Coke	2 oz	40–60 mg
Milk chocolate	1 oz	6 mg
Dark chocolate	1 oz	20 mg

Females get drunk faster than males, not only because of their smaller size but also because they have only about half as much of the enzyme 'alcohol dehydrogenase' that breaks down alcohol in the stomach before it enters the bloodstream. This enzyme helps prevent us from getting really drunk and damaging our livers. In other words, the way one drink affects a female is the same as the way two drinks affect a male. Men drinking a pint while women drink a half therefore makes a lot of sense. Females also remain drunk for longer than males.

Many young people are surprised to learn that alcohol is a depressant. If they are feeling low and have a few drinks there is a risk that they will feel even worse the next day. Alcohol also depresses your brain's activity, so as well as making us feel unhappy and depressed it can seriously affect our ability to concentrate. This can have a highly deleterious effect on young people's school work. Alcohol also depletes Vitamin B levels, alters blood sugar and raises blood pressure. All of these things can make us feel under strain. Mixing drink with drugs is extremely dangerous and potentially lethal. The combination can make people vomit in their sleep and cause suffocation.

SUMMARY

Drinking too much can cause many problems, including mood swings and even relationship problems. Drinking also

- is a physically addictive drug producing withdrawal symptoms which can be fatal
- can lead to violent behaviour

- reduces inhibitions, and can lead to risk taking behaviour, which has long-term consequences for the young person
- can kill by alcohol poisoning
- kills brain cells; research in the US has shown that a large number of teenagers drink enough to affect their school performance
- multiplies the cancer-causing effects of smoking.

It is important to help young people feel confident to make their own decisions about drinking and not to drink just to fit in with the crowd. They should feel they are not missing out on anything, that by not drinking they may have more energy to enjoy themselves and will look better too.

To help young people to tell when their drinking is becoming a problem you can ask the following questions:

- Do they drink because they have a problem or to help them face up to stressful situations?
- Do they drink when they get angry with others?
- Do they prefer to drink alone rather than with other people?
- Is their drinking affecting their work?
- Do they get into trouble when they are drinking?
- Do they often get drunk when they drink, even though they don't mean to?

These questions will help form the basis for frank discussions around the role of drinking in the young person's life.

Fat

The reason why women often have more *body fat* than males is because, in prehistoric times when there was not a lot of food available, they needed to have extra energy stored to feed themselves and their babies. A woman must also be a healthy weight to menstruate and give birth. Men had more muscle and less fat due to the activity involved in searching for food. This is one reason why dieting often does not work, as when you cut your food intake dramatically, your body responds as if there were a threat of starvation. It slows down your metabolism (the rate at which the body burns up calories), and stores as much spare fat as possible. A moderate intake of fat is necessary for lots of things including skin and hair maintenance, body temperature maintenance and cell functioning. Many people's diets contain too much fat.

How to reduce fat in the diet

Fat in the diet can be easily reduced by choosing low fat products, switching from saturated fats like butter to polyunsaturated fats, such as olive or sunflower oil, and cutting down on fried foods, and grilling or boiling instead.

When the level of glucose in your blood is low, you tend to feel hungry. *Snack foods* that contain refined carbohydrates and sugars are quickly digested. However, the brief boost in blood glucose is quickly followed by a fall in blood glucose levels so that we feel hungry again very soon after. This may lead to more snacking, is an easy habit to fall into, and can lead to weight gain. If your meal is balanced, that is, contains other nutritional elements as well as carbohydrates, the food is more slowly digested and absorbed and it should be some time before you feel ready for the next meal.

Dieting and eating disorders

Dieting and eating disorders are on the increase for both young males and females. To tackle these, we first need to understand the reasons behind their onset. For some young people, these reasons may be deep-seated and need a good deal of therapeutic intervention to come to terms with. Other young people may benefit from open discussions around cultural assumptions of weight and success.

You can ask young people whether they are happy with their body shape, whether they believe that thin women have more friends, are happier and more successful, and what sources of reference they use when thinking about their ideal body weight (e.g. magazines, friends, television, family), and what causes people to diet or develop unhealthy eating patterns.

Age 14 to 16 is the most vulnerable period for the onset of eating disorders, although they can start as early as 9 years old. Anorexia peaks between 14 and 18 years. The mortality rate for anorexia is 10%. Theories explaining its onset vary. Low self-esteem has been linked to eating disorders together with having an external locus of control, whereby one tends to feel out of control, helpless and depressed. Family climate may be an indicator where families are seen as rigid, enmeshed, with no appropriate conflict resolution, and where self-reliance and self-sufficiency are not encouraged.

The figures for eating disorders and dieting in adolescent girls have risen sharply in the past few years. There are strong cross-cultural differences; for example, the international mean rate of anorexia is one in 100,000; however, a recent study of white, middle-class girls' schools in Britain found the rate to be one in 1,000. The medical effects of bulimia include loss of tooth enamel, menstrual irregularity, oesophogeal tears, gastric rupture and cardiac arrhythmias. Only 10% of anorexics are male. Medical consequences include amenorrhoea (cessation of periods), reduced cognitive function, cortical atrophy, non-normal production of neuro-transmitters, hypotension, possibility of heart failure, constipation and osteoporosis.

Weight and body shape

Many young people today, particularly young women, express dissatisfaction with their appearance and body shape. This appears to be affecting girls at a younger age than ever before. Many female role models are thin, and the desire to be thin has made dieting in adolescence a common occurrence. The diet industry is worth approximately £21 billion a year and has a lot to gain from projecting images of slim models having a happy and successful lifestyle. Women's magazines, television, cinema and the music industry are all involved in selling the myth that happiness and being thin go hand in hand.

It is a good idea to open a discussion with young people on the subject of weight by exploring these basic assumptions. Ask young people to bring along some of the magazines they read, or a picture of their favourite pop artists or actors. You will recognize that almost every girl photographed is very slim with a beautiful face. They never show photographs of a plain, unhappy, thin girl, so we tend to associate thinness with attractiveness and happiness.

Discuss the effect that these pictures have on the young people. Do they make them want to buy the product? Do they automatically believe that these people are happy? If so, these pictures have done their job in manipulating insecurities and stimulating desires. Acknowledging that this is the sole purpose of these images is the first stage in undermining their truth or realism.

There is a growing concern about the effect that all these magazines, pop and television images are having on the health of women. Girls as young as 9 are now going on diets in order to be as skinny as these 'role models'. This is dangerous, as it will interfere with normal growth and development, both physically and psychologically. Diets also affect metabolism and can ultimately lead to weight gain. It is estimated that 95% of people who go on a diet end up the same weight or even put on weight within a year. Young girls and teenagers who diet may prevent their bones from growing normally and can impede the production of oestrogen (which makes skin soft and hair shiny). Dieting can also lead to depression.

It is estimated that at present, a quarter of all women are on a diet. Approximately nine out of ten women express dissatisfaction with their body shape. This is obviously having an impact on teenage girls. There has been a large increase in the number of people with serious eating disorders. If dieting begins in young girls, it is eight times more likely to lead to anorexia or bulimia, which can be fatal. There have been calls from researchers, medics and professionals working with young people to persuade the media to display more realistic images of female bodies.

Does being slim bring happiness?
It is worthwhile exploring with young people if they really believe that slim women are happier. The truth is that many slim girls are unhappy.

Are slim girls more attractive?
It is now a well-known fact that when men and women are asked to choose a figure they find most attractive in women, women always choose a thinner figure than men. If you are holding this discussion with a mixed group, you could ask the male members of the group to talk about a girlfriend, or someone they find attractive, and ask them to say why. Usually, a woman's personality, smile, eyes, sense of humour, hair, intelligence, voice, posture, interests and confidence will be just as important as her figure.

If a girl is always dieting she can become less attractive to her peers. She may appear vain and self-obsessed, she might not be much fun to be around, or seem very interested in other people. If she appears dissatisfied with her appearance, boys may be influenced by this and also think less of her. Dieting removes the shine from girls' eyes, hair and skin, giving a lack-lustre appearance. Dieting can take energy away, thus making a girl lose her sense of humour and self-confidence. She may become depressed.

Our relationship with food
It is often the case that while boys simply eat food, girls have a relationship with food. Many young women feel guilty if they think they've eaten too much. Food can become something they want to control, or an enemy that they must battle against. Appetite can be affected by emotions. Feeling depressed or stressed can cause us to eat less or more than usual.

Eating disorders may be a way of avoiding other issues by focusing on food, a way of coping when life becomes too difficult, or a way of feeling more in control. They may be caused by family issues, dieting, emotional problems, adolescence, societal pressure to be slim, genetic factors or sexual abuse.

Eating disorders can have serious consequences including:

- Depression, due to chemical changes in the brain.
- Difficulty in concentrating or thinking clearly as brain cells do not have enough nutrition to function normally.
- Brittle bones which can dissolve and break easily.
- Broken sleep.
- Risk of attempting suicide.
- Vomiting produces acid which can burn away tooth enamel. The salivary glands in the neck can become swollen, leading to puffiness in the face.
- Laxatives can produce constant stomach pains, swollen fingers and constipation.

The effects of dieting
Dieting messes up our metabolism and, when young people decide to eat normally again, they may find they gain weight quickly. It can lead to bingeing as it confuses their natural appetite and will make them crave fattening foods. Severe weight loss leads to hormonal imbalances which can cause facial hair growth in girls. Girls who are obsessed with food will miss out on so many other important aspects of life and often feel tired, irritable and under pressure.

The best way to lose weight
Try to encourage young people to maintain a well-balanced, low fat, high fibre diet and also to eat breakfast. This speeds up the metabolism and will give them energy throughout the day. It also reduces the need to eat snacks which are high in fat later on.

When eating becomes a problem
Try asking young people: Is their weight below normal? Have they ever tried dieting to lose weight? Have they stopped menstruating? Have people commented that they look thin? Do they think about avoiding food all the time? Do they feel a little obsessive about their intake of calories? Do they binge and make themselves vomit, or use laxatives to lose weight? Are they secretive about eating? If they answer 'yes' to any of these questions, they may have an eating problem. You should suggest that they talk to their parents about this. Possible options will include counselling for them or with their family, joining a support group, or seeing their GP.

Exercise[2]

To begin this discussion, start by asking young people the following questions. They can comment on their exercise diaries or on an average week. How much exercise did they take this week? How much exercise do they usually take? What types of exercise do they enjoy? Do they feel they get enough exercise? How do they feel after they have exercised? How do they feel when they don't exercise? What do they feel are the benefits? What are the obstacles? What would make it easier?

What is exercise?

Exercise should not be seen just as a PE class or having to go through the pain of an aerobics class. Exercise should be seen as physical activity which should be a natural part of living life to the full. Dancing, walking, running, swimming, cycling, soccer, tennis and rollerblading are examples of aerobic exercises.

Why exercise?

There are so many reasons for advising young people to take plenty of exercise. Mentally, it will reduce stress, improve their performance at school, improve concentration and memory, lift depression, improve self-confidence and even enhance creativity. Physically, it improves self-image, boosts energy levels, lowers body fat, improves general health, boosts the immune system, improves quality of sleep, and reduces physical tension. It affects behaviour by reducing hostility and irritability.

WHY DOES EXERCISE MAKE YOU FEEL GOOD?

- Exercise causes the brain and spinal cord to produce their own powerful opium-related drugs called endorphins. These enhance mood because they have a chemical make-up similar to opium-based drugs, and explain why people feel a 'high' after exercise, particularly aerobic-type exercise, like running, dancing, aerobics, soccer and so on. This is why people enjoy dancing until they're tired and sweaty – lots of aerobic movement and a hard, steady beat.

- Exercising will make young people feel more attractive as it improves their *self-image* of their body.

- It reduces and prevents *depression* by lifting mood. Participating in sports can also give young people a sense of team spirit and achievement. It allows them to forget about their worries and focus on the moment.

- *Stress* and nervousness are dramatically reduced by the chemical effects of exercise. Physical activity neutralizes the stress hormones that make you jittery and leaves you feeling more balanced. Physical activity relaxes your muscles which also allows you to feel more calm. Going for a run before a stressful event, like an exam, can relieve much nervousness and stress.

- Research has shown that *mental performance* on IQ tests improves greatly following just twenty minutes of aerobic exercise. Physical activity improves alertness and the speed at which we think.

Why is exercise good for you?
As well as keeping us healthy and slim, exercise helps to build up muscles, increase energy, prevent heart disease and increase longevity. It improves our immune system because running is interpreted by the body as a sign that we may be in danger. The body therefore goes about boosting the immune system and creating more natural killer cells. This is why those who are physically active suffer less from colds.

When exercising, young people should

- Do at least twenty minutes of aerobic activity at least three times a week. This means increasing your heart rate and breathing.
- Keep active! Walk or cycle to school or a friend's house instead of taking the bus, help out with housework, go dancing.
- Exercise should not become a new, more acceptable form of diet addiction; its aim is to make people healthier and a side-effect will be a better body shape.
- When you are aerobically fit you have more 'fat-burning compartments' inside your muscles. This keeps you burning fat a lot of the time and means that if you continue to eat normally, you will burn more calories than you take in. Exercise controls your appetite and makes you less likely to crave unhealthy foods.

- Muscle is a 'hungry' tissue: 450 grams of muscle burns thirty to fifty calories a day just doing nothing, while the same weight of body fat burns only two. So the more muscles you have the more calories and fat you burn, even when you're just sitting down.

Why not exercise?

It is easy to come up with excuses for not exercising, even when we are aware of all the benefits. Excuses which should sound familiar are feeling too tired, not having enough time, being too busy, feeling self-conscious, feeling too fat (or too slim, so don't need it), or that it's boring.

Making exercise a part of life

Young people should be encouraged to think of *physical activity* rather than 'exercise'. They should try to incorporate it into their routine. They should choose different types of exercise for different days, keep active during the day, and make sure they choose convenient times and places to exercise. It's a good idea to make exercise sociable (e.g. by joining team sports). This creates incentives as young people can meet up with others, and they will feel they are letting others down if they don't show up. If they are not enjoying PE, you could suggest that they talk to their PE teacher about more fun ways to exercise.

Sleep

Sleeping well is central to coping with life, managing stress and having positive feelings of well-being. Sometimes it is difficult to know whether we have a sleep problem, as everyone needs different amounts of sleep. Ask young people how they slept during the last week. Do they feel they get enough sleep? Do they regularly feel tired throughout the day? Does sleepiness interfere with their daily activities?

Experiencing poor sleep quality can make us feel miserable, irritable and unable to cope. It is therefore an important stress management tool for young people to learn how much sleep they need, and to try to get this. There are three main kinds of problem: difficulty falling asleep, wakefulness during the night, and waking too early in the morning. Many people think they have a sleeping problem, when they are actually underestimating how much sleep they get.

Although sleep needs vary greatly, most young people need about nine hours' sleep a night. They may need more around exam time. If they miss one night's sleep, this should not affect them too much. A change in sleep routine will take a few weeks to get used to. Losing even one hour's sleep in a night can affect concentration the next day. Feeling depressed, lacking exercise, eating poorly and worrying can affect sleep quality. Taking sleeping tablets is a major cause of insomnia and should be discouraged in young people.

The part of your body that requires sleep the most is your brain. The rest of you can get by without it as long as you get enough rest and food. There are two main types of sleep: 'deep' sleep and 'light' (REM) sleep. The first of these revitalizes your brain and the second is when dreams occur. If young people are not getting enough sleep you can suggest the following tips.

IMPROVING SLEEP QUALITY

- Accept that whatever sleep you do get will be of benefit, enjoyable and restful, and do not fret about how much sleep you're getting.

- Try to go to bed at the same time every night and always set an alarm when you need to wake up at a certain time; otherwise sleep can be disturbed as you worry about waking.

- Do not indulge in weekend sleep binges that disturb this routine.

- Try relaxation exercises about an hour before bed.

- Take regular exercise.

- Do not eat heavy meals or take drinks containing caffeine before bed.

- Try taking warm milk or warm malt drinks before bed.

- Avoid taking sleeping tablets as these ultimately exacerbate sleep difficulties.

Other tips include making sure the bed and bedroom are comfortable, urinating before going to sleep, and avoiding alcohol.

Having a relaxing evening routine can help people with sleeping difficulties. Doing something calm, like watching television, reading or having a bath, allows the mind to settle and relax. Warm milk contains a mild sedative that some people find helpful. Exercising, studying, playing very active video games or watching anything disturbing on television might contribute to difficulty in getting to sleep.

Getting up earlier in the morning can sometimes do the trick in making people tired enough to fall asleep in the evening. If young people report difficulty in getting to sleep, suggest they stick to the same routine every day and forgo weekend sleep-ins, as these confuse the body clock. For most teenagers these are a normal part of catching up on sleep. If they regularly wake early, you could also suggest that they do something productive or enjoyable during this time (like reading or making plans). This will stop them getting frustrated and dreading this time.

If young people are having difficulty in sleeping, encourage them to learn relaxation skills. They can try being stern when worries enter their head, and refusing to follow these thoughts. They can also try progressive relaxation exercises, counting sheep, counting breaths or visualizing relaxing places. The main thing for them to remember is that few problems are solved in the early hours of the morning. A good idea is to write down the things that are bothering them, and decide to look at this list again in the morning.

Learning how to relax

Try asking the young people the following questions: Do they find it hard to relax? What things do they do to help them to relax? Do they suffer from muscle tension? What is the hardest thing about becoming relaxed? Do they feel stressed because they are too relaxed? How would they advise others to relax? Are there any unhealthy ways of relaxing? What would be the biggest benefits of learning to relax? Have they become more skilled in identifying their own personal stress response? Do they use a stress diary?

Living life in a relaxed way is a philosophy, a habit, a skill and a way of life. First, it has to be an outlook on life; being calm and laid back. It is also a skill that can be learned, i.e. being aware of our body; knowing when our muscles are tensed up, and learning to let the tension go through mental and physical exercises. It is also a routine, i.e. getting into the habit of sustaining a calm lifestyle and learning to react to stress in a particular way. It is a way of caring for yourself by replacing energy resources that are being used up all the time. Developing relaxed attitudes and habits is the best way to prevent stress in your life. Quite simply, relaxation is all about letting go.

Why should young people learn how to relax?

Perhaps young people don't want to relax. They may find the idea boring or think it means leading a less exciting or fulfilling life. A useful exercise is to ask young people to tense up their body and their face really tight and to think of a list of things they need to do. Then ask them to stand up and shake out all the tension and to take some deep breaths. Then ask them to make a list. Ask them which way was easier. This exercise usually dispels the belief that being tense makes us think more efficiently.

The important thing to convey is that learning coping skills and how to take things in our stride will actually allow us to lead an even fuller life with more energy to enjoy it. For some people, relaxing is an automatic skill. Others need to learn techniques. These all centre around being aware of the way we react to situations both physically and mentally and learning to stay relaxed. Being aware of muscle tension and following through with breathing and stretching exercises is often a first step. It is often interesting to suggest that young people relax their shoulders. They may not have realized that their shoulders were tense.

Tension brings pain and discomfort, often in the neck, back and shoulders. It can also lead to tension headaches. Having tense muscles can make us feel even more stressed, and can lead to anxiety about the aches and pains. Getting into the habit of relaxing or 'dropping' our shoulders is a fast relaxation strategy. Young people will be surprised how often they need to relax them. Having tense muscles can also make us tired (as tense muscles are working muscles) and irritable (as your body is feeding back to your mind that you are under stress). This is a waste of energy that could be used better. Muscular tension can be found in people with specific attitudes. For example, a female student who believes that no matter how hard she studies she is bound to fail her exams may experience chronic neck tension and pain, while a male student experiencing a lot of anxiety about the future may develop chronic stomach problems.

Learning to relax involves keeping an eye on posture, not rushing around, making time to do relaxing and enjoyable things, creating options so that we don't worry too much about things not working out, taking breaks, and finding a quiet time everyday. Young people could also try listening to a relaxation tape, taking a hot bath, burning some scented candles, having someone rub their feet or back or going for a walk. Sleep, exercise, rest, eating properly, humour, pleasure, relationships and time management can also help us relax.

Breathing

There are two types of breathing: chest breathing and abdominal or stomach breathing. Suggest that young people place a hand on their stomach and a hand on their chest to find out which way they are breathing at any one point in time.

Chest breathing

This type of breathing is useful when we are undergoing vigorous exercise but is inappropriate for ordinary, everyday activity. It is part of the 'fight-or-flight' response and consists of shallow, jerky, unsteady breaths. When we are feeling stressed or anxious, the mind interprets this as a threat and activates this response to enable you to run. However, today, many people experience ongoing levels of anxiety and stress and so are in a constant state of chest breathing, although they are unaware of this. The effect of this, paradoxically is to maintain feelings of anxiety in a vicious circle. Until chest breathing is replaced by deep, even and steady diaphragmatic breathing, all efforts to relax the body, nerves and mind will be ineffective.

Abdominal breathing

This is the most efficient way of breathing in terms of the amount of oxygen you take in. If we actively practise breathing from our stomach, together with mental and physical relaxation, we can bring down our blood pressure and reduce feelings of stress leaving us feeling more calm, composed and able to cope. The advantages of abdominal breathing are that it gives the body enough oxygen, it expels carbon dioxide adequately (unlike chest breathing), it relaxes the body and mind and it improves circulation to abdominal organs (which aids digestion and protects against ulcers).

PROGRESSIVE RELAXATION

This exercise is a popular relaxation method and can be done during the day or evening to relax, or to aid sleep.

- Sit upright and comfortably in a chair. Close your eyes without squeezing them tightly.

- When you are comfortable, curl and clench your toes and tense your feet as hard as feels comfortable. Hold this for a few moments and then breathe out and let the tension go. Stretch out your feet and feel them relax.

- Now breathe in and tense your legs and thighs as hard as feels comfortable. Hold it for a few seconds and as you breathe out feel the tension being released.

- Breathe in again and as you do tense your stomach by pushing it out – hold this tension for a few seconds then breathe out and relax.

- Move to your chest, and as you breathe in feel your chest expand – hold this expanded position for a few minutes and then relax and breathe out.

- As you breathe in, tense your back, particularly in between your shoulder blades. Hold the tension for a few seconds and then release it as you breathe out.

- Now tense the whole upper half of your body – feel the tension – breathe out and let go of the tension and relax.

- Tense your shoulders by lifting them up towards your ears as you breathe in – hold for a few seconds and relax, and drop the shoulders as you breathe out.

- Clench your fists as tightly as possible and experience the tension in your hands and arms. Hold the tension. Now let it go and shake out the arms and hands.

- Move your attention to your head and face. Scrunch up your face, tightening up all your facial muscles – hold the tension – then release it, relax and let go as you breathe out. Breathe in and yawn with open mouth and raised eyebrows. Hold for a second and release and let go.

- Stay seated for a few minutes and focus your attention on your breathing, allowing the breath to become slow, deep and even.

Pre-menstrual syndrome

The Professor of Human Metabolism at the University of London describes premenstrual syndrome (PMS) as the world's most common disease, yet there is still no agreement among doctors about the best way to treat it. There are over 150 different symptoms, and it affects teenagers as well as older women. Symptoms include irritability, anxiety, depression and fatigue. Even as early as the ancient Greeks, Hippocrates noted the symptoms of agitation and lethargy associated with blood trying to escape from the body. There are several reasons why PMS may be affecting more women today than in the past: these include fewer pregnancies, stress, diet and the contraceptive pill. It is also likely that we are more aware of this condition nowadays.

The organization of reproduction in women is carried out at the *menstrual controlling centre* in the hypothalamus at the base of the brain. This is a part of the brain which also contains the controlling centres for day/night rhythm, weight and mood control. Although we are still not sure what the exact causes of PMS are, we do know what helps to alleviate it.

Coping with PMS

- *Diet* has been argued to be the most important way of reducing PMS. Young people should be advised to avoid sugar at this time, as it can cause a sharp drop in sugar levels after a while, making them feel cranky or tired and crave sweet things. In addition, if they find that caffeine makes them feel tense, agitated, anxious or interferes with their sleep, they would be well advised to cut down on caffeine before and during their premenstrual time. According to Dr Katharina Dalton, a leading researcher in the field, the strongest influence on PMS is low blood sugar levels, caused by an inadequate diet. She claims that during this period, the timing between meals or snacks is extremely important – i.e. there should never be a gap of more than three hours (except when we are asleep). She recommends eating a starchy snack every three hours. Finally, we still don't know whether the bloating associated with PMS is due to excess salt, but some researchers recommend cutting down on salt during this time. Dr Dalton believes that it is lack of regular starch and not salt that results in bloatedness.
- *Coping skills*: By charting their good and bad days on a menstrual chart, young women can learn when their most vulnerable times are. They can then take extra care of themselves at these times, for example, by resting more, using relaxation, or taking mild exercise, like walking.
- *Avoidance tactics*: Young people should try to be aware of when their symptoms are at their worst and not plan anything difficult for this time. Factors which make PMS worse include tiredness, hunger, stress, alcohol and smoking, so they should be advised to avoid these if they can.
- *Stress* is not the direct cause of PMS, but it does make it worse and we may be least able to cope at this time. Stress and PMS naturally aggravate each other.
- They should avoid working very late at night. The controlling centre for the day/night rhythm is situated in the hypothalamus, at the base of the brain adjacent to the

menstrual controlling centre, so any disturbance to the day/night rhythm centre upsets the menstrual hormones. The effect is very like jet lag, when our biological clock is disturbed.

- They should make sure they get enough *rest*. If they suffer from PMS they will need a full eight hours' rest in bed. Lack of rest results in irritability and tiredness. If they can't sleep, lying resting in bed is just as effective.

- *Exercise*: There is a world of difference between everyday physical exertion and beneficial exercise. To be beneficial, exercise must be sufficiently prolonged to increase the pulse rate for some minutes after exercise has stopped. This could be twenty minutes of aerobic activity, like brisk walking, jogging, cycling or tennis. Exercise is invigorating, increasing the circulation of blood and oxygen consumption, which helps to release tension, and premenstrual aggression.

- They should cut down on *alcohol*. Even small amounts of alcohol make PMS worse. When alcohol is taken it interferes with the normal action of progesterone in brain chemistry, which may exacerbate any feelings of depression they are already experiencing. PMS sufferers will also find that they are not able to take nearly as much alcohol as at other times without becoming intoxicated.

- For some women, the contraceptive pill can alleviate the symptoms of premenstrual tension.

- Other forms of treatment include relaxation skills, assertiveness training (see Chapter 5) and evening primrose oil (although the evidence is very controversial on this).

CONCLUSION

This aim of this chapter is to help you to pinpoint the important relationship between physical health and feelings of strain. To do this, it is recommended that you:

- discuss normal eating, sleeping, exercise and drinking routines

- explore the way these habits affect thoughts, feelings and behaviour

- explain the role that nutrients, sleep quality and physical activity play in mental health

- discuss the problems that excessive drinking can cause
- explore the myth that slim equals happy
- explain the health hazards of dieting
- discuss the benefits of exercising and potential obstacles
- discuss the importance of relaxation, breathing and stretching
- suggest ways of coping with premenstrual syndrome.

As Chapter 4 deals with homework and study, you could try asking young people in advance to make a list of what the biggest problems are for them as regards studying and what they find helps them to work better.

Notes

1 Sigman, A. (1992) *Getting Physical – A Teenage Health Guide*. London: BBC Books.
2 Ibid.

CHAPTER 4

Study skills and time management

Stress appears to be hitting people at increasingly younger ages because of the more complicated and competing demands being placed upon them. Our society, more than ever, is pushing the importance of success, achievement and winning. While teenagers may feel they have more opportunities than their parents, they may also feel they must take these opportunities and succeed more than ever. We're made to believe that the more successful job you have the happier you will be. A postman is more unhappy than a brain surgeon or a pop star, which of course is not the case.

It can be difficult to help young people to put their exams into the right perspective. On the one hand, as an adult with their best interests at heart, you will want to encourage young people to achieve the best they can and you will know the consequences of not achieving well at school. On the other hand, exam stress and pressures at school have been shown to contribute significantly to adolescent stress, sometimes to such a degree as to adversely affect the young person's ability to do well. There are also more opportunities available today to people who want to repeat exams, try alternative educational careers or pursue options which are not solely dependent on academic results.

The key is to help young people achieve their best at school while at the same time nurturing their self-esteem, self-confidence and mental health, and acknowledging that the teen years are difficult enough without young people feeling undue pressure and stress. To do this, you need to be able to help them develop essential study skills, time management and relaxation skills. This will help them to work efficiently, to 'switch off' when they're not working and to keep things in perspective. Informing them of the range of options available to them in their future career is essential so that they do not panic if the option they're pursuing doesn't work out.

Sessions on study skills and exam preparation have always proved highly popular. The advice and tips are usually of immediate benefit to secondary school students as well as young people pursuing other courses that require application. While it is important to relay these guidelines, it is also important for students to be able to give each other advice on what works for them, and this can be encouraged within the discussion time. Although this chapter, more than any of the others, is related to school and may involve you if you're a teacher, the same effort should be made to sustain a relaxed atmosphere, or 'time out' from normal classes. This will encourage students to raise issues and to feel that the discussion is as much to do with their well-being as their exam performance.

Talking to young people about studying

It is usually a good idea to ask students in a group setting to suggest what, for them, are the main obstacles and problems with studying. It is helpful for most young people to realize that others share their concerns and difficulties. Students should be asked whether there are further issues they would like to discuss, as the obstacles to studying can vary. If these issues haven't been adequately addressed by the end of the discussion, invite students to bring this to your attention so that they can be explored and potential solutions discussed.

Divide the students into groups of four, and elect a spokesperson for each group. Ask them for feedback to the overall group.

- What are the main problems regarding homework, studying and keeping up with course work?
- What feelings and obstacles arise regarding study habits?
- What do they feel is the most difficult part of studying?

Study skills[1]

Studying for exams is one of the most stressful and difficult challenges young people have to face. Some people seem to be better able to manage their time, and cope with homework and revision demands. It is more than likely that rather than being 'more intelligent', these people have simply learned to use effective study skills to help them to get the work done without becoming too bogged down in it and feeling helpless and depressed. This chapter aims to provide ideas and techniques to help young people to improve their study routines and to make the time in which they do study more productive. Many of these tips are relevant for any activity that requires them putting their mind to something, like learning a new skill, a musical instrument or writing fiction.

- *Input:output*: The most important study technique is to invest time in study. No amount of study tips will allow them to escape the fact that the more time they spend working, the more they will learn and achieve.
- *Getting started*: Many find it hard to get down to study. In fact, a lot of people say that this is the most difficult part. You can ask your students whether this is true for them. Identifying that this is the hardest part of study is important, as they can then focus their efforts on this aspect.

Being able to get down to work is the true divider between those who get a lot out of study and those who don't. When people find they can't get down to work they don't get as much done and produce stress for themselves. They are neither relaxed nor working. This achieves nothing. Students should make starting work as pleasant as possible. Once they begin they'll usually discover that the work is less awful than they imagined it would be!

Making it easy

1 *Where they study*
Wherever the student studies should be made as attractive and comfortable as possible. They should try to work in the one place each time (e.g. their room). This will help them to keep things organized. Keeping their desk tidy and free of unnecessary clutter is also a good idea, as it will help them to feel in control and focused and will not turn them off studying.

2 *How they study*
Listing what they have to do is essential for efficient studying. Students should always write down what they want to get out of their study session before they start. It is a good idea to prepare a schedule for the amount of time and incorporate breaks into this. This is also a good idea, as a common excuse is that we don't know what to do or where to start as we have so much to do. Not knowing what to do can make it easy to not do anything. In addition, ticking things off a list will give them a sense of progress as they work through the items.

3 *Why they study*

Everyone loses motivation sometimes when they are working towards something. A good idea for students is to write down their reasons for working and what they hope to achieve in the short and long term.

Making it enjoyable
Body clocks

It may not be possible for young people to choose the time of day when they study. Equally, they may not feel that this is important. However, research has shown that some people concentrate better at certain times of the day, i.e. mornings, afternoons or evenings. If they notice a difference in how productive their work is at different times, it is a good idea to work around this. This may be relevant at weekends when they have more control over when they work. They should use the time to study when their concentration is at its best and then not to feel guilty relaxing at other times. However, it is important to remember that exams don't take place at night, and developing a habit of working late may not help them to perform on the day.

Taking breaks

If we felt when we sat down to study that we had to stay there for hours, it would be a huge disincentive to even begin. Having realistic chunks of study planned before they sit down will help students to get down to work. Concentration is best when we stick to chunks of about forty-five minutes with ten- to fifteen-minute breaks in between. If breaks are timetabled in, students won't feel guilty about taking them and will stick to their schedule.

A change is as good as a rest

It is usually easier to study when we choose several different subjects to look at in one session. In addition, large projects broken down into smaller chunks are far less intimidating and more enjoyable to work on.

Finishing the study period
A tidy desk is a tidy mind

Taking a couple of minutes to store and file study materials at the end of each session is important. It makes it easier to begin the next session and cuts down on time-wasting while looking for notes. It is often an unconscious excuse to potter around the room without getting down to study. Convince students that time spent at their desk should be time spent working, which will leave more time for guilt-free relaxation and recreation afterwards.

Use a carrot!

The oldest trick in the book is rewarding ourselves for doing things we'd prefer not to do. This is especially true for studying. If we associate studying with treats, we will find it easier the next time. Ask students to think of ways they can reward themselves for studying. For example, if they spend their Saturday afternoon studying, they might decide to treat themselves to a night out. Even after completing small chunks of work, it is a good idea to give themselves a small reward. This could be watching their favourite television programme, going for a walk, making a phone call, eating something they like or a soak in the bath, but only if they get everything done that they had planned.

Students should be imaginative in what treats they use and not stick to the old favourites of chocolate and television. This way, they are giving themselves something to look forward to *and* getting the work done! Treats must come after the work is done. Students can try asking parents or teachers to provide some rewards based on the amount of study they do. Ask students to think about things they would really like to do, such as music lessons, driving lessons or simply having a friend over. These can be used as incentives.

Make it social

As this book hopes to show, discussing issues aids learning and the absorption of information. For students, this can be an effective study tool if it helps them to work through the material and explain it in their own words. This is an excellent memory device. If they can talk to a friend about the work, it means they are more likely to remember it. Working with others also makes studying more enjoyable. Suggest that they choose a topic to revise with a friend (on their own) and then get together to talk about it. Some of us find it impossible to work when we have good company around, however, and if this is the case it is advised that they try to work efficiently on their own and arrange to meet their friend later.

Spread the word

Ask students to ask their friends what tips they might have for making study easier.

Health and studying[2]

Body clocks and sleep

The concentration required by studying requires that our body clocks are not disturbed. This means going to bed at the same time every night, getting up at the same time every morning and getting enough daylight. If we confuse our body clock we feel sluggish, sleepy and our concentration is poor. We are unlikely to do productive work. We also find it difficult to remember the material we read at these times. Young people, as a rule, require more sleep than adults, up to nine hours or more, particularly coming up to or during exam time. Regular sleep patterns, and plenty of daylight and fresh air are therefore recommended. Suggest that students study near a window and take lots of breaks outside. It is also worthwhile reminding young people that if they get into the habit of working late at night, they are (1) less likely to take in the material, (2) at risk of making going to sleep difficult, and (3) less likely to remember the material during the exam which will take place during the day.

Physical activity

Students who are fairly fit tend to do better at their schoolwork. Recent research has also proved that doing twenty minutes of aerobic exercise will have an immediate positive effect on performance in IQ tests, feelings of stress and anxiety, alertness and concentration, accurate and quick thought processes, memory and learning, and creative thinking.

Aerobic exercise is any exercise which makes our heart beat faster and our breathing rate increase. This means any activity using the large groups of muscles, particularly in the legs, for example: jogging, fast walking, cycling, swimming or dancing. The key is to increase your heart rate and rate of breathing and to keep it there for at least twenty minutes. When you do this, your brain releases endorphins which influence the way you think and feel. The endorphin 'high' you get from this will immediately improve your brain's capacity to think creatively and make decisions.

Advise students to do some aerobic exercise three times a week, especially coming up to an exam, and to do a little aerobic exercise immediately before the exam. They can also try walking rather than taking a lift, or go for a twenty-minute jog. This is particularly useful before an afternoon exam, where they might otherwise feel a little drowsy after lunch.

Nutrition
Blood sugar

Our ability to concentrate is very quickly influenced by the level of glucose or blood sugar in our bloodstream. If this falls we feel less alert, find it hard to make decisions, concentrate or remember things. We can also feel tired, low, irritable and sometimes hostile. Try asking young people to suggest possible causes for dips in blood sugar levels.

Blood sugar levels dip when young people go on diets or skip meals, particularly breakfast. Levels also fall, paradoxically, when we eat or drink things with too much sugar. This is because normal foods provide enough sugar for the body, and so when we consume foods and drinks which contain too much processed sugar, the body reacts by lowering the level of sugar circulating in the bloodstream. We often end up feeling tired and sluggish which can make us crave sweet things, so a vicious circle ensues. Sugar produces serotonin, which can cause fatigue.

Getting into the habit of eating breakfast, particularly before an exam, and eating regular healthy snacks and meals will help keep blood sugar levels stable. Eating breakfast will also stop them getting hungry mid-morning and going for a sugary, unhealthy snack. While eating complex carbohydrates is healthy, eating a lot at lunch-time can lead to sluggishness.

Glucose sports drinks, glucose tablets and sweets also lead ultimately to drops in blood sugar levels which can inhibit concentration and make us feel tired.

Caffeine

Try asking young people, if they drink coffee when doing homework or studying, how many cups of coffee they usually drink, if they feel that coffee is a good way to help them concentrate and what drinks or food contain caffeine.

Caffeinated drinks are often used to help provide stimulation coming up to an exam and to keep students awake. However, going for a walk, having a shower or taking a break are far more effective. Caffeine though providing short-term stimulation, actually lowers blood sugar levels after a short time, producing tiredness. It is well known to lead to edginess, and can make young people feel more nervous and stressed out about their exams.

Alcohol

Alcohol, antihistamines and cannabis all affect alertness, so students should be advised to avoid these before studying and the night before an exam if they want to be at their best. Alcohol kills brain cells. In addition, if they need to take medication (for instance, if they have hay fever, or a cold or flu) some medications (including some night-time cold remedies) contain alcohol or antihistamines which can cause drowsiness the following day.

Television and music
These can affect concentration, and students should be encouraged to avoid them while studying or to choose undemanding programmes that do not vie for their attention.

Organizing the study area
Advise young people to study in the same place and to ensure that this is a bright, tidy, quiet and organized place.

Reading material

Advise students to:

- *Prepare.* Look through the text to get a sense of the main subject areas, the way the material is broken down, interesting pieces, how it fits in with what they already know.

- *Get an overview.* Students should read any summaries or conclusions in the material. This will help them to reread the chapter or book and be clear about what they are looking for in terms of its main messages.

- *More detailed reading.* Students should be encouraged not to give up if they cannot follow the text. They should read on to see if the following chapters will help them to understand it. Students should be encouraged to raise difficulties with the teacher, and be assured that everyone finds some texts difficult. This may be the fault of the author or the intrinsic difficulty of the material.

- *Review.* It is always a good idea for students to consolidate what they have learned by going back and organizing the material. Students could set up their own categories or simply reflect on how the material is presented. A good approach is to study for thirty-five minutes and then review what they have read.

- *Test.* Nothing will help students remember what they have read more than testing themselves. Jotting down a few questions, taking a break and coming back to see what they remember is an excellent memory strategy.

Taking notes
The most important thing for students to remember when they are taking notes is that, for the notes to be useful and aid memory, they

must be actively processed by the student. They should not just be passive recordings of the original. Students should digest and organize the material in their own individual way, i.e. in a way that makes sense to them. This does not have to make sense to others and there is no right or wrong way of doing it. What is important is that the notes reflect the way the student has received and processed the information.

Condensing versions of notes is a good way of revising and can prove helpful to look at before going into exams. Being able to condense notes means that the student has come to terms with the content of the material and is able to make choices about the key elements.

Students may sometimes need advice about how to take notes and may benefit from an exercise on note-taking in class. You could give them a photocopied chapter or even a newspaper article and ask them to underline or highlight the key points, to condense the text and to try to organize it in an easy to remember way. This is an essential study skill. Even reading with a pencil in their hands, prepared to mark pieces of text which are confusing or interesting, will help keep them alert and processing the material.

Exams
Prioritize
It is impossible to try to study everything. Students need to choose which topics they have to cover and concentrate on these. If they have trouble choosing topics, they can ask a teacher to help them. It is useful to continue summarizing the information as they approach the exam, so that by the time they enter the exam they only have a few keywords on a card. These will trigger memory of the wider material to be remembered.

Mock exams
These are an excellent way of seeing how much information students can remember, discovering their strengths and weaknesses, and practising their exam timing. They can give themselves mock exams at home. Trying to remember something in a mock exam and failing provides a good incentive to go back to the material to see what they forgot, and they are less likely to forget this again. Practising answering exam questions is a good way to reduce anxiety.

Designing a study timetable
Students should write a list of all the subjects they are doing and prioritize them in terms of the ones which they know least about to the ones they know most about. They then need to draw up a timetable

and focus on the subjects they know least about, while at the same time revising topics they are confident about, so as to prevent feelings of panic and anxiety. Encourage students to keep the work well organized with each subject in its own folder.

Exam stress
Coming up to an exam

It is normal for students to worry before an exam, but it is important to convert the worry into action and get focused. Students will find their minds filling with thoughts about all the things that could go wrong. You need to impress upon them that just because these thoughts are recurrent, they are not realistic. Assure students that they are normal reactions and just the result of the pressure they have been under to do well. You can assure them that their teachers and examiners want them to do well.

Encourage students to take a *deep breath* or to try counting to ten to relax when they go into an exam. They need to read the *instructions* carefully and read the exam paper through to the end. Writing *short notes* at the beginning on the questions they are going to answer may stop them feeling anxious about not knowing enough to write. This is also good for jogging the memory. Encourage them to *adapt* what they know to the questions and to keep their answers relevant.

REMEMBER WRITES

- Use your best Writing
- Try to Relax
- Read the Instructions and questions properly
- Time each question strictly
- Have Everything you need with you
- Write Short notes first

Stress and worry
Keep it in perspective

Although it can be hard, it is good to advise students to try not to worry too much about the exams, as this will not help their performance. They should focus on sticking to their study timetables. Staying focused and organized rather than getting caught up in worrying will help them to do their best in their exams. There have been suicides linked to exam stress, and although achieving well at school is good for young people's future, you may not realize how anxious and stressed they are until it is too late. Young people can spend a lot of time worrying about the consequences of their exams, thinking about what course they will get into, what kind of job they'll get, whether they'll be satisfied, how much money they'll earn, or if their parents or friends will approve. Assure them that they can only do their best and it is not the end of the world if things don't go entirely as planned.

It is worth reminding them that stress and worry take up a lot of time and energy which would be better applied to the task at hand. Advise them that if they feel their anxieties about the exams are interfering with their work or the rest of their life, they should definitely find someone to talk to about it. Make sure that students are aware of counselling facilities both within the school and locally.

If young people feel that their parents have unrealistic expectations for them and are placing too much pressure on them to succeed, they should discuss this with them. If you, as a concerned adult, have witnessed signs of anxiety which could be debilitating, it may be worth your offering to facilitate such a discussion. If the young person cannot talk to their parents, and feels uncomfortable talking to a counsellor or guidance counsellor, perhaps they could try talking to a relative, family friend, brother or sister. They could even ask them to talk to their parents. The main thing is to encourage and inspire without causing undue stress and impeding their performance. In other words, support and guidance are more effective than provoking anxiety *per se*.

Time management

Try asking young people what they think time management is. Do they think they have a problem with time management?

The symptoms of poor time management include a sense of being rushed and hurried all the time, being late regularly, feeling low in energy and motivation, feeling like you're always trying to catch up, feeling irritated and impatient, not getting things done, being indecisive about what to do next, and always putting things off.

The central principle of time management is to spend your time doing those things you value or those things that help you to achieve your goals. But what are our goals and what do we value? Most people would admit to spending a great deal of time involved in activities which they neither value nor help them to achieve their goals. Try asking young people to think of these types of activities. Why is this? It is easy to think that it is because we are weak-willed, or lazy or inefficient. But often the real reason is that we are unclear about our values and goals.

Exercise on time management

This exercise will assist young people in identifying their highest priorities. Ask them to close their eyes and imagine their own funeral. What would they like people to say about them? What would they like their friends, family, teachers or classmates to say? You can then explore with them what this exercise says about the sorts of things that are important to them. For young people, as with older people, this exercise often helps to clarify what values are important to them, and will help them to decide if they are living their lives in a way that is in keeping with these values. It can help them to see what kind of person they want to be, and what they want to achieve.

We often want to be remembered as being a good friend, a loving son or daughter, someone who was there to listen, or as someone who was cheerful. We also like the people we respect to respect us too, and to respect what we are trying to achieve.

Knowing more about our values and goals can help us to plan a life around what we believe in. Suggest that students use a pie chart to design how they would like to divide their spare time. It may take a while to become clear about what their values are.

How to manage time well

> *Procrastination is the thief of time.*
> Edward Young.

Once your students are clear about what they value in life and what they would like to achieve, they will be good time managers if they never put off studying and thus spend time in limbo between working and relaxing; get into a routine that allows them to waste the least time hanging about; feel confident in their choices and follow through on that; break down large projects into smaller ones, thus making them less intimidating; accept that they won't be good at everything but this is no reason not to enjoy things; and set aside time to plan each week.

If your students are finding it hard to manage their time, suggest that they think about what's important in life, set goals to achieve this, write down an action plan, and set about fulfilling this in an organized way. Encourage your students to estimate how much time they spend per day on various activities by keeping a diary or time log. They may

not have realized quite how many television programmes they watch
or telephone conversations they make.

CONCLUSION

Preparing for exams can cause significant stress for many young
people. In this chapter it was suggested that you:

- talk about the pressure to succeed and where this comes from

- ask them if it is affecting their well-being

- discuss difficulties getting down to study or putting in
  sufficient time

- discuss where, how and why they study

- offer advice on study skills

- discuss the role of nutrition and exercise in effective studying

- offer advice on taking notes and exam preparation

- reassure them on the importance of keeping things in
  perspective

- engage them in exercises on time management.

Notes

1 Butler, G. and Hope, T. (1995) *The Mental Fitness Guide: Manage Your Mind*.
  Oxford: Oxford University Press.
2 Sigman, A. (1992) *Getting Physical – A Teenage Health Guide*. London: BBC
  Books.

CHAPTER 5

Interpersonal and communication skills

This chapter is about relationships, paradoxically one of the biggest causes and comforts in the stress process. Relationships form a central component in the stress process at all ages. Having people in our lives who provide emotional, physical and material support as well as advice can buffer the effects of stressful events. As they move from early to late adolescence, young people place increasing importance on peer support and approval. This is highly important and provides a forum for young people to discuss the multitude of novel thoughts and experiences through which they are journeying. Parents, relations, teachers, sports coaches and other significant adults in their lives are also hugely important in providing guidance, love and support during this vulnerable transition.

Unfortunately, when we are under stress we can become more difficult to be around; we can become irritable, distant or simply not there. This chapter aims to help you to communicate to young people that although they may find their relationships difficult they are probably their most important support and resource for combating stress. Students should be encouraged to discuss which relationships are particularly difficult for them and the ways in which they are stressful. There are suggested discussion points which should prove interesting and thought-provoking for young people. As with all discussions around stress and coping, it is useful for you to ask the young people to raise the issues first and form the discussion around a response to these issues. Ask them to think about the main problems they encounter in their relationships. Ask them to think specifically about their relationships with family, friends, teachers, other adults, boyfriends or girlfriends.

When you ask young people to list things that cause them stress, they are often quick to mention 'people stress', i.e. those individuals, be they parents, teachers, friends or classmates that are a source of conflict for them. Everyone has times when they feel down or annoyed by the actions of others. We feel they have behaved inconsiderately, aggressively or inappropriately. Unfortunately, these are often the people we see every day at school, at home or at work.

A useful exercise is to ask young people to think of five people who cause them the most stress or hassle. Give them a couple of minutes. Then ask them to think of the five people to whom they turn when they are under stress. Give them a couple of minutes. Now ask them if they found that there were at least one or two of the same people in both categories.

It usually comes as something of a revelation to young people that they rely so heavily on the very people who cause them the most stress. This is true for most of us, as relationships with parents, brothers and sisters, friends, boyfriends or girlfriends can cause real pain as well as bringing us joy.

Investing in relationships is important in order to help us maintain our mood and well-being and in helping us to cope with day-to-day events. It is highly important that young people are encouraged to draw on this support, as many stressful life events they have encountered and will encounter in the future can be eased through social support and advice. The suggestions contained in the rest of this chapter are aimed at ameliorating relations between young people and others. Reducing conflict and day-to-day tension through learning self-awareness, negotiation, assertiveness and listening skills can make it easier for young people to feel confident in turning to those relationships at times of stress.

Central to this book's message is that stress is about the way we view the world as well as our objective circumstances. Therefore, when it comes to people in their lives who are 'stressing them out', young people can learn to assume responsibility for their half in that relationship as they bring with them their own views, emotions and actions. Interactions with others often cause us to feel threatened, angry or upset, and we react in the same 'fight-or-flight' way described in Chapter 1. This rarely improves the situation.

Based on their personality and life experiences as well as their current circumstances, many young people show patterns in the way they deal with conflict with other people. Some young people will do anything to avoid confrontation. They are inclined to conceal their feelings from others and seek to appease them. They often blame themselves for breakdowns in the relationship. Others hide deep-seated feelings of insecurity by creating conflict. They can bully and act insensitively and are often unaware of how this comes across to others.

Relationships[1]

Ask students to think of a relationship which is causing them stress. Then ask them to think of something that would improve this relationship. Give them a few minutes. Ask them if they thought the relationship would improve if the other person changed their behaviour or attitude.

It is normal for both teenagers and adults to assume that if other people change, their relationships will improve. We usually think 'if my boyfriend would stop doing this' or 'if my mother wouldn't do that' things would be better. This seems obvious to us. However, by placing the onus for change on the other person we are, in fact, doing ourselves a disservice. We are losing our control on our own relationship and well-being. We are handing over that control to another person which means taking power away from ourselves. The important thing to communicate is that to improve our relationships we can only change ourselves. Others will then change the ways in which they relate to us.

Feeling confident enough to 'be ourselves' in a relationship can be difficult for all of us, but particularly for young people who are in the process of identity formation. You can discuss this with young people if they find it difficult. It is in fact the key to a good relationship. They will recognize that the relationships in which they feel they can be themselves are the ones in which they feel most comfortable, confident and happy. This does not mean that they can behave exactly as they wish if it means being rude or hurting other people. It also does not mean that they should always feel totally comfortable, because sometimes we learn a lot in relationships that are challenging. It just means that when we feel that others accept us we can express ourselves, and often the relationship is more satisfying as a result.

But how do we start thinking about our relationships, and how can we start to change them?

In adulthood we relate differently to different people, and this is particularly true for young people as any parent or adult working with young people knows. They can often be difficult with adults while friendly and cooperative with peers. Ask young people to think about a relationship which is causing them stress or sadness and to ask themselves when do they feel at their worst in these relationships and when do they feel at their best. Ask them if they have noticed patterns in terms of what happens in their relationships. These are crucial questions in helping them to work out what is going on in their interactions with different people.

Being aware of how we tend to respond to people and situations is a useful skill. Most of us have developed habitual ways of responding over time and may not even be conscious that we are acting routinely in a particular way. If young people can become aware of these tendencies they will be in a better position to decide whether reacting this way is helpful, healthy or brings them happiness in their lives. An example might be if some aspect of their work or appearance is criticized and they react as if their whole being has been attacked. They feel undermined, angry or worthless. Another example is if someone fails to make contact having arranged to do so, and they feel rejected and isolated.

These are normal reactions that don't tend to last for too long. If, however, they respond very strongly in this way every time this happens and the feelings last for some time, it is likely that they have developed a pattern of response. This can come from experiences in the past and usually reflects their view of themselves and their insecurities. However, it can be damaging to new relationships and stop them leading fulfilling lives. Being aware of our patterns of behaviour is the first step in analysing and deciding where they come from, whether they are rational and whether we want to change them.

Think about it

Try to encourage young people to think about problems within a relationship in specific terms rather than having vague feelings of discomfort. If there are unresolved issues, difficult emotions or feelings of dislike, then these will be easier to work through if they are clearly identified.

Take responsibility

As already mentioned, taking their fair share of responsibility within the relationship will give young people more freedom and control. This means that they don't allow others to make all the decisions, but rather that they participate, that they don't respond to others with aggression and that they don't place blame without acknowledging their own part in the relationship. Learning to be flexible and responsive is important to stop them getting stuck in habitual ways of behaving which can prove hard to break.

Watch how others change

You can suggest that young people try the following exercise. They can decide to change their behaviour towards a person who is causing them a great deal of stress. If they normally ignore this person, they can try being more attentive to what that person is saying and doing. If they normally act in a withdrawn and submissive manner, they can try being assertive and tell the person calmly how they feel. People may not respond in the way they would like, but at least they will be able to see that the relationship is not outside their control.

Solitude

Although relationships are important to our well-being, we should remember that spending time alone can also be a fulfilling and worthwhile experience. Many of the things we produce and of which we are most proud happen when we are alone, such as working on a project. Other things like listening to music can be even more enjoyable when we are alone. If we are at ease with ourselves, we will be at ease with others. Keeping a diary can be good for letting off steam and thinking about things which are important to us, particularly for teenagers.

SUMMARY

Developing healthy relationships means that we need to acknowledge that:

- We can only bring about changes in others by changing ourselves and changing the way we relate to them. We can change the way we behave around and towards them, the way we feel and think about them, and the way we express affection or anger.

- We have to give changes time to take effect. This is particularly true in relationships where there are more people involved.

Suggest that young people think about the sorts of things that always make them react strongly or perhaps unreasonably. This may tell them more about themselves or their past relationships than the current situation. Ask them to think about why the situation makes them angry and where this might come from.

Communication skills

It is difficult for many of us to express the way we feel. This can be particularly hard for teenagers who may feel self-conscious about what they want to say. They may feel too unsupported or angry to discuss things which are important to them. It could be argued that young men find this particularly difficult, but it varies greatly in both young men and women. Not being able to express how we feel can be stressful for many reasons. It can mean that others don't know what we want, that it is hard to get help when we are having trouble coping with a problem, and that, when we feel sad, we cannot talk about ways of feeling better. It can also lead to misunderstandings in our relationships.

Assertiveness

Feeling unable to assert ourselves can be very stressful because all the feelings which are not expressed can build up, making us hostile or resentful. They can also explode in bursts of anger or crying. Sometimes these feelings are stored up for a long time and are a source of silent hurt. None of these ways of coping with our feelings is good for our well-being.

Adults as well as teenagers often misinterpret the meaning of the term *assertiveness*. Try asking young people to define what it means to be assertive. Do they see themselves as assertive? Whom do they know who they would define as assertive and why? What often emerges in these conversations is that we are confusing assertive with aggressive behaviour. We think of people who insist on having their own way the whole time or who have a pushy manner as being assertive. In addition, adults may sometimes be afraid to talk to young people about being assertive as they fear it will make them more demanding or aggressive.

What is assertiveness?

The fact is that these assumptions are untrue. Assertiveness is really about being *fair to ourselves and fair to others*. Assertiveness means realizing that our needs, wants and feelings are neither more nor less important than those of other people, but rather they are equally important. This means that when we tell people about our needs, we should be open and accurate and not exaggerate. We are assertive when we stand up for our rights in such a way that the rights of other people are not taken away. When we behave assertively we are less likely to leave situations feeling bad about ourselves or leaving others feeling bad. Young people who are confident and assertive are more able to stand up to peer pressure, to relate democratically to others, to be self-aware and aware of others. They are more likely to see relationships as systems.

Why be assertive?

Being assertive means being able to ask for what you want, to express your likes, dislikes and interests freely, to talk about yourself without self-consciousness, to accept compliments, to disagree politely, to say no and to be relaxed around other people. Being assertive is half-way between being passive and being aggressive and, as with coping skills training, often requires thinking about things in a different way. You can discuss the following basic tenets of assertiveness with young people. These include the right to make mistakes, say no, express hurt and pain, not have to justify themselves to their friends, and to be alone. Do they feel they have these rights?

The bottom line is that young people are entitled to their own feelings and opinions. If they value themselves and trust their own feelings, they will feel more confident in expressing themselves regardless of whether their friends feel and think differently. This is an invaluable tool throughout life. They will probably even find that when they have confidence in themselves and start valuing themselves, other people will start to value them more and have more confidence in them. The trick is to stop worrying about whether other people like them and start focusing on being fair instead. The rest will fall into place.

All they need to remember is that being assertive is all about balancing their needs and the needs of others.

Negotiation skills

Negotiation forms a large part of all relationships throughout life. During the teenage years, young people must negotiate with parents, siblings, teachers, friends, boyfriends and girlfriends on a multitude of issues, including leisure time, pocket money, choice of friends, choice of boy/girlfriends, choice of school subjects, holidays and so on. Negotiation is a useful skill for young people to learn, not because it will teach them how to get more out of situations, but rather because it will teach them the rules of cooperation, to see responsibilities as linked to rights, the importance of trust as well as 'give and take' in relationships.

You can suggest to young people that in future circumstances which require negotiation or cooperation they try to:

- Be clear when they express themselves to avoid misunderstandings.

- See the situation from the other person's perspective.
- Be constructive – placing blame is rarely a positive way to proceed, so move on from where you are at.
- Accept responsibility – it is rarely helpful to start a discussion on the defensive or on the moral high ground. Suggest that they acknowledge their contribution to the argument or situation before moving on, even if they are only acknowledging it to themselves.
- Recognize individuality: different individuals become upset about different things or take different things in their stride. Similarly, some people need a good deal of intimacy while others need space, some people like to talk about their feelings while others prefer to remain silent.
- Think about how they would like to be treated in this situation and act this way – if they'd like understanding and warmth, then try to give this.
- Better out than in – it's a bad habit to allow themselves to bottle things up. Reports indicate that repressing emotions has all sorts of negative effects on our mental and physical health. Young men in particular need to hear that it is acceptable to talk about the way they feel.
- Keep a lid on insults – these usually cause arguments to escalate.
- Count to ten or go for a walk if they're getting angry. Anger rarely achieves anything in discussions. If they have grievances these should be expressed in a calm and constructive way that helps to change the situation.

In summary, good negotiation involves finding out what each person wants, trying to find the common ground, looking for alternatives that allow both parties to get what they want, being flexible and trying to give and take as much as possible. It is important that young people learn to be clear in how they communicate. This means expressing how one feels rather than retreating to a room to brood. This will help others see that they are hurt or angry.

It is worth discussing the assumption held by some young people that conflict with parents is inevitable. Although it is natural and often healthy for teenagers to argue with their parents while discussing differences of opinion over values, rules and so on, it is not necessarily inevitable. They may be surprised to learn that their parents would often rather work things out amicably and look for the common ground.

Listen!

Being a good listener is just as important as being listened to. Learning the importance of listening will help young people to provide support to others, making them more likely to receive social support when they need it. It will help them to understand where other people are coming from and so lessen the risk of misunderstandings, arguments and communication breakdowns. It will help them to show others that they care about them and so help nurture their relationships. It will also help them to learn from others.

> You can suggest the following to young people to get them started on improving their listening skills:
>
> - Make it clear to others that they are listening by using important signals such as looking straight at the person who is talking, maintaining eye contact, nodding or saying 'uh-huh'.
>
> - Give simple feedback to show they are listening by acknowledging what the other person is saying; for example, 'did you really?', 'is that right?'
>
> - Summarize what the person has said to show they understand; for example, 'so you'll have to go back in then?'

These are easy ways to show we are listening. When discussions get heated we are less inclined to listen. However, learning to listen in these situations is a useful negotiating skill for young people to learn.

> Suggest that they:
>
> - Listen until the person is finished, as the end of their point might be different to what was expected.
>
> - Articulate their agreement as well as their disagreement. If we fail to do this the speaker assumes we feel differently and can become agitated trying to get their message through.
>
> - Be open – our assumptions of what someone wants out of a conversation can be different from theirs. Allow people to express themselves.
>
> - Try to understand the real meaning of what people are saying, not just the words. People's tone of voice and body language can express different sentiments from what is actually said; for example, when someone says, smiling, 'about time you

got here!', it may be meant as a light-hearted joke but could be taken as a criticism or attack.

Listening skills, in conjunction with assertiveness and a knowledge of the importance of social support, will help young people to get the most out of their relationships.

Social support

Many studies have shown that talking to people about how we feel can help us feel better. Simply expressing our feelings as well as engaging the advice and support of others is a hugely important way of managing stress.

As well as being a source of enjoyment and fun, relationships are a resource when we feel stressed. They can, however, be a resource we don't use, because the relationship is the problem, or because stress has made us feel too tired to talk or because we are reluctant to express our worries. When we are under pressure we often put a strain on our relationships and may not be aware we are doing this. This is commonly known as 'taking it out on others'.

Ask young people to think about those who can give them support when they need it. Ask them to think about whether, when they are under stress, they usually explain this clearly to the person, or tell them exactly how they are feeling. Is it possible that they have been expecting the other person to ask them first? Suggest in future they take the first step and tell these people when they are under pressure, and enable them to be supportive. Ask them to think about whether they have been irritable with those close to them, because of feelings of pressure and strain. If this is the case, it may be helpful to say they are sorry and to explain that their behaviour was not because of them, but because of the strain they are feeling.

Quite simply, young people need to know that they need other people around to help when they are feeling stressed, and so acting with hostility will deprive them of this resource. Suggest they find other ways to let off steam, like exercise, music, dancing, sports or keeping a diary. The most important thing is that they spend time with other people and don't cut themselves off, that they learn to talk about their problems and how they feel, that they spend time with people who care about them and respect them, ask for advice, tell people why they're feeling cranky and try to help others when they too are under pressure.

Bullying

Begin the discussion by asking young people to define bullying. Can it be verbal as well as physical? Are boys more likely than girls to bully or do they bully in different ways? Is there a particular age when bullying is more common? What should friends or classmates do when they witness bullying? What should teachers or parents do when they discover bullying? What would their advice be to others if they are being bullied?

Bullying is more commonplace than many people imagine. The figures produced by the Anti-Bullying Centre at Trinity College Dublin suggest that in Ireland 31% of primary and 16% of secondary school students had been bullied at some time. This amounts to nearly 200,000 children at risk of experiencing bullying. In the UK, two out of ten boys and three out of seven girls reported being bullied, from sometimes to often.

Bullies can be people at school, people they don't know, friends with whom they've fallen out, brothers or sisters, or adults. Being bullied can be very hard to cope with and can make young people feel sad, helpless, angry or scared. Young people should be aware that no one should have to put up with being bullied. A lot of people don't tell anyone because they are frightened, depressed or don't think anyone else can help. They might even feel that it is their own fault. Their self-esteem suffers, and every day becomes a battle to get through.

Bullying can be verbal or physical. It can be psychological when friends choose to ignore others and cut them out of the group. A young person might find themselves bullied because others are jealous, perceive him or her as different or because they refuse to go along with certain things. Usually, young people fear that if they tell on the bully, the situation will become much worse. They are often afraid that other people will see them as cowards, tell-tales or simply won't believe them.

It is important to assure young people that most teachers are trained to deal with these types of situations. They can talk through with them the different options they both feel are appropriate. You should encourage them to tell their parents, whose experience and insights will help them to cope better with the situation. Adults can advise them on a whole range of possible strategies. In addition, the bullies will have their own difficulties, and alerting adults to their behaviour may help them to address their own situations. In summary, if young people are being bullied, they need to take action using the advice of adults whom they respect and can talk to.

Why intervene?

Adults may sometimes feel that if they intervene they will undermine the victim, somehow retard their growth of coping skills or disturb their relationships with their peers. However, the consequences of bullying are too extreme to adopt a *laissez-faire* attitude. In recent years more research and initiatives have focused on bullying, in part because of severe cases linked to bullying, some of which have even led to suicides. Bullying is caused by aggressive behaviour which if unchecked in childhood can be sustained into adulthood. This can mean that violent, aggressive behaviour is carried over from one generation to the next. Failing to act can give a silent but powerful message that aggressive, violent or abusive behaviour is appropriate and acceptable. Parents may feel torn between reporting bullying to the school and following their own child's wishes, and so teachers may not always expect to learn about bullying from a child's parents.

When to intervene
Bullying has been defined as 'a repeated aggression, verbal, psychological or physical, conducted by an individual or group against others'.[2] Bullying is found in males and females of all ages and socioeconomic backgrounds. It can be short or long term but can always cause a great deal of distress to the victims. Teachers, parents and others can look out for bullying in the following symptoms: reduced ability to concentrate, poor or deteriorating work, fear of going to school or work, loss of confidence and self-esteem, aggressive behaviour, depression, anxiety, wanting to leave school or job, or attempted suicide.

How to intervene
It can be difficult for those caring for children to identify when and where bullying is taking place and sometimes to know what to do when they have discovered its occurrence. Many schools have now developed a bullying strategy and teachers will have been informed of this. This is essential in order to help teachers identify and tackle bullying. If promoted actively it will give a clear message to parents and students that bullying is regarded as a serious issue and not a 'natural part of growing up'. It will warn potential bullies of the consequences, and it will educate parents so that they know more about the causes of bullying and what to do when it occurs. It will help teachers to act within a recognized and appropriate framework of response.

The following recommendations refer to appropriate school actions where bullying has been identified.[3]

- Investigate the problem and take reports of bullying seriously.
- Respond to every incident, no matter how minor, and act immediately.

- Keep a careful eye out for bullying at high-risk times, such as break times, the beginning and end of the school day and when students are changing for sports.
- Monitor high-risk students, those who are likely to be targeted; these students may be different in some way, may keep to themselves or appear not 'to fit in'.
- Make sure that locations where bullying is likely to occur are monitored carefully. These include poorly lit corridors, cloakrooms, changing rooms, school yards and bike sheds.
- Try assigning particular teachers in turn to watch out for bullying.
- Reinforce non-aggressive behaviour by rewarding students who show caring behaviour.
- Educate students by showing a video or giving a presentation on bullying. Portray the bully as someone with difficulties and inadequacies to remove any status they might otherwise gain from bullying. Encourage students to report when they or others are being bullied. Assure them that they will be believed and helped and that confidentiality will be respected.
- Be supportive to other staff, set up a system to deal with bullying, talk to other staff about their own experiences of bullying in adulthood.
- If someone confides in you that they are being bullied, assure them that you believe them and take this seriously, that you will help and that the situation will end.
- Counselling is sometimes necessary for students who have been the victim of serious bullying. Discuss this with the child's parents.
- Discuss the situation with the parents of both the victim and the bully. Talk about possible causes for the behaviour and ways the children can address the problem. Causes of bullying can include experience of abuse and violence, poor coping skills, low self-esteem, not being able to keep up at school, parents being over-strict or being bullied by others.
- Always focus on the behaviour of the bullies and not the bullies themselves. Suggest more effective coping skills.
- When bullying takes place in groups, confront each of the bullies on their own. Help them to understand their own role and responsibility.
- Expect bullies to compensate the victim for anything broken or taken. Expect them to apologize.
- In serious cases of bullying, if parents refuse to cooperate invite external advisers and assessors to participate.

It is important to educate young people in defining bullying. They may not realize that they are experiencing bullying and may therefore fail to take appropriate action. If young people are being pressured to act in a particular way, to do things that they don't want to do, are being called names, teased, insulted, threatened, robbed or beaten up, these are all different types of bullying.

In summary, bullying is a serious, physically threatening and psychologically damaging occurrence that can interfere with healthy adolescent development and cause severe problems to young people at a vulnerable stage in their lives. Always be concerned, and act when you learn of such episodes.

CONCLUSION

Relationships cause considerable stress in adolescence as in adulthood. They are also often the best stress management resource we have. To encourage young people to maintain healthy relationships, it was recommended that you:

- ask them to recall difficulties they have experienced with people in their lives

- ask them to consider whether the relationships that cause the most stress are also the ones they turn to in difficult times

- discuss the importance of relationships

- persuade them to accept responsibility for their own role in their relationships

- encourage them to 'be themselves'

- ask them to look for patterns in their relationships that might be rooted in the past

- discuss the good and bad things about being alone

- ask them what they think being assertive means

- discuss how being assertive can help them in their relationships

- provide them with advice on negotiation and listening skills

- convey the importance of talking to others when they are feeling upset or down

- discuss bullying.

As the next chapter is about self-confidence, it is often useful to suggest to young people that they do some research on the subject prior to your discussion. Ask them to ask ten people whether they consider themselves to be self-confident, and to ask some people whom they think are self-confident if they consider themselves to be self-confident, and if there are things they are not confident about.

Notes
1 Butler, G. and Hope, T. (1995) *The Mental Fitness Guide: Manage Your Mind*. Oxford: Oxford University Press.
2 ABC – Research and Resource Unit, Teacher Education Department, Trinity College Dublin.
3 Copley, B. and Williams, G. (1995) *The Teenage Years: Understanding 18-20 year olds*. London: The Tavistock Clinic.

CHAPTER 6

Treating yourself right

No amount of skills, strategies, ideas and information on learning to cope with stress will be of any use unless young people (1) value themselves, and (2) have the self-confidence to put these into effect.

Treats

'All work and no play . . .' has long been an adage which suggests how limiting and stultifying it can be when we deny ourselves playtime and enjoyment. In order to develop as rounded, happy people we all need to give ourselves rewards and to 'treat ourselves right'. Treats do not necessarily have to be things which aren't good for you. They are simply a recognition of efforts we have made and the need for us to take breaks in order to remain relaxed and stress-free.

Whelan (1993) talks about sources of energy in much the same way that we talk about treats. These sources differ for each of us and you can ask young people to think of things that make them feel happy, fulfilled and relaxed. These could include going dancing, spending time with friends, watching a video, listening to a favourite CD, going for a walk or taking a bath. Whatever our own sources of energy or 'treats', these allow us to continue to thrive and cope with life in a positive and constructive way. They somehow combat what can be referred to as energy drains, such as having too much work, strict deadlines, not spending enough time outdoors, arguments with friends or family, rejections, or things going wrong generally.

When you ask young people to think of treats, encourage them to think of treats which are just as good for them in the long as in the short term. Frequent drinking, smoking, eating fast foods or staying up all night are likely to leave them twice as drained, as their health will suffer and their energy levels decline. Similarly, acting inconsiderately, while it may bring short-term pleasure, may end up bringing them more stress in the medium term. Feeling happy, creative and well nurtured in turn gives us the energy to get stuck into other tasks like school work, projects, maintaining difficult relationships and so on. It's all a question of balance.

Ask young people to:

- Think about a difficult task they are facing and to plan a treat for having finished it. This works for small tasks too; young people can learn to associate one hour's study with half an hour's treat, such as chatting on the phone, watching television or just relaxing.
- Introduce the treat immediately after the task is completed to maximize the effect. This works well for studying and will make it easier to concentrate. It can work for other difficult situations, such as having to discuss a sensitive issue with someone. They can plan a swim or a video for afterwards.
- Think of small, regular treats that are harmless pleasure.
- Do the things they dread first to get them over and done with. Utilize the energy that comes with beginning a project to do the difficult parts first.
- Use the things they like doing as rewards. For example, if they're planning to go bowling, they could squeeze in some study time before they go rather than have to face it when they get back.

Boosting self-confidence

Try asking young people:

- What they think self-confidence is.
- What they think the symptoms of low self-confidence are.
- What they feel self-confident about.
- What they feel low in self-confidence about.
- Were they surprised by any of the responses to their survey of self-confidence?
- Did the people that they thought were self-confident consider themselves to be self-confident?
- Were there things that they were not confident about? Did that surprise them?
- Did they feel that other people have more self-confidence than them?
- How can they tell if somebody is confident or not?
- Are confident people always confident? Or confident about everything?

Low self-confidence can have a pervasive effect on a young person's life. Their thoughts, behaviour, feelings and the way they hold themselves are all affected. Having low levels of confidence can be a major obstacle for young people trying to live their lives. As the group 'The Smiths' put it, 'Shyness can stop you doing all the things in life you want to.'

Although it is normal for us all to feel lacking in confidence at some time, for young people this can be especially difficult, and a good discussion on self-confidence should help debunk a few myths and flesh out the area. It's a good idea to suggest that the questions you raise are also discussed with peers. The following is a list of the main ways that a lack of self-confidence affects us. These are experienced by everyone from time to time, but for some people they can seriously impede them from achieving things that they value. Try asking young people to think about which of these things is true for them.

Low self-confidence[1]

When young people feel low in self-confidence they tell themselves they can't do anything, they're not good enough, things are too difficult, they don't know how, they can't cope, and that they won't be any good. They feel apprehensive, nervous, anxious, stressed out, worried about difficult things that are coming up, frustrated and angry with themselves for not doing things better, afraid of the unknown and new situations, resentful of other people who find things easy, and disappointed and low.

They may be more withdrawn, keep a low profile, find it hard to make suggestions or put themselves forward, put things off, avoid taking on anything new or making changes in their lives. They may stoop, retreat into themselves, avoid looking people in the eye, fumble and fidget, have tense muscles, and feel tired.

Confidence is complicated

Confidence consists of many things. Suggest to the young people that they ask themselves what they are confident about and what they are not confident about. For example, they may be good drivers but bad at English essays, they may be good at fixing cars or minding children, but bad at maths. They will soon realize that there are things on both sides. In addition, without exception, confident people always have something they are not confident about. Suggest they ask someone whom they consider confident what they are insecure about. There will always be something. The lesson is to focus on the positive.

Seeing is deceiving

An important thing to communicate is how many people who appear confident are actually not so. What they are actually successfully doing is giving the appearance that they are confident. This is a good trick and one they can learn, because once we start behaving confidently, we often begin to feel more confident too. Their interviewees will always be able to think of something that makes them feel unsure of themselves. In fact the majority of people feel less confident than they appear.

Practice makes perfect

Wouldn't it be great if we always did everything right? Or would it? Most of our valuable lessons come from the mistakes we have made along the way. This is true for everyone. Young people should learn to believe that what's important is trying new things, learning and growing, and not the mistakes. Once they've been practising for a while, they'll improve at most things and their confidence will grow. Perhaps they might even see their mistakes as equipping them with funny stories to share with their friends. They should remember that they won't be the first to be in this situation, or the last. Try asking them to think of something they can do now that they couldn't do before.

Confidence in five easy steps?

1 If at first . . .

Suggest that if they are unsure about starting out on something, they give it their best shot for a while and see what happens. Ask them to think about the first time they tried to ride a bike or use a computer.

2 Talk the talk and walk the walk

It is amazing how emulating characteristics tends to trick our brain. If young people were even to try to pretend to be confident in stressful situations, their confidence levels would actually grow. Ask them to think of someone confident whom they know and respect and to consider how he or she would act in this situation. As everything is interrelated, any changes in our posture, thoughts, feelings or behaviour will influence each other and they will immediately begin to feel more confident.

3 Learn and move on!

We all tend to remember our mistakes in a negative light, but young people lacking in self-confidence can focus excessively on appearing foolish or feeling inadequate. An important lesson for life is to try to think about what we learned from the experience. Ask them to think of a mistake they have made and what they learned from this. There is no mistake that hasn't been made before, and it is only people who are afraid to try new things who do not make mistakes.

4 Don't beat yourself up!
There is nothing to be achieved from beating ourselves up having made a mistake. Once the situation is in the past and we have learned from it, we need to move on and not allow ourselves to be dragged down by the experience.

5 Be nice to yourself
If we don't give ourselves the same breaks as we give others we care for, our confidence levels will never grow. Young people should 'cut themselves some slack' and forgive themselves for their mistakes.

Boosting self-esteem[2]
Self-esteem is about how we see ourselves. It is a core aspect of our very being, often based on our childhood and adolescent experiences. It is central and inseparable from the way we handle events in our lives and how we feel about ourselves all the time. If we have high self-esteem we feel good about ourselves and when it's low we will feel bad about ourselves. Self-esteem is something that needs to be nurtured over time and it develops throughout our lives. It allows us to value ourselves and feel that our contributions are worthwhile. There are, however, things we can do to help increase our self-esteem. Young people cannot have enough self-esteem, as it brings not arrogance but real security. It's probably the best stress management tool there is.

Be the devil's advocate
When we suffer from low self-esteem we tend to be dismissive towards ourselves. We see ourselves as worthless and unliked. If we could only be rational and look at the evidence, we would often find it difficult to maintain this viewpoint. Suggest that young people, when they are feeling negative towards themselves, try to fight the bias and focus on their good points and acknowledge that they matter.

If you're the hardest judge that you could get – tell yourself to get real!
Statements which some young people will find familiar include: 'I'm unwanted', 'they don't like me', 'I'm in the way', 'I don't matter'. They can learn to recognize that these statements stem from feelings of low self-esteem, which does not make them true. Similarly, we often

acknowledge the achievements of others while dismissing our own, by saying they mean nothing or we were just lucky. If we tend to be critical about ourselves we can expect things to go wrong, which is unhelpful in facing challenges. If things don't go well, we can use this as evidence that we can't cope or aren't popular. In some ways these are self-fulfilling prophecies. Once they recognize that these voices are irrational, young people can gain the confidence to tell them to shut up.

All you can do is your best
There is a big difference between wanting to do well and torturing yourself when you don't do well all the time. Sometimes when our self-esteem is low, we make rules that are hard to stick to as they are unrealistic and impossible. Examples of this are:

- I have to get things right all the time
- I should always come first in the class
- I must always win at sports
- I'm not good enough
- Boys should never look weak
- I can't make a mistake
- If they realize I lack confidence, they won't want anything to do with me
- I shouldn't talk about it when things go wrong
- I can't change.

If we repeat these unfair generalized comments to ourselves all the time, we'll just feel bad about ourselves. Ask young people to think about what they may be saying to themselves which is undermining their self-esteem. Remind them that they can only do their best.

Nurture company that nurtures
Throughout our lives, but particularly in adolescence, we can be around people who undermine our sense of self-worth. If young people feel their self-esteem is low, ask them to make a list of the people who help them to feel good about themselves. Who are the people who make them feel bad about themselves? Suggest they spend more time with the former and in general avoid friends who undermine their confidence.

Self-esteem changes all the time. We all feel better about ourselves some days than others. Remembering this in itself is a worthwhile skill, as we can ride the bad days more easily. The most important thing is to be kind to ourselves and value ourselves.

Unhappiness and depression

> *It is an illusion that youth is happy,*
> *an illusion of those who have lost it.*
> W. Somerset Maugham.

The relationship between depression and stress is highly complicated. Stressful life events as well as poor coping skills can lead to depression, and feelings of depression can create stress in the lives of young people through loss of social support and creating stressful events.

Many adolescents go through periods of sadness from time to time. For some, this can be more serious and depression may follow. Depression is a highly complex condition. It may be due to genetic, biochemical or hormonal predispositions, or rooted in early or current relationships and experiences. This section provides advice for helping young people who report feelings of unhappiness. It is important, however, that you are aware of sources of professional help and can provide young people with contact details of counsellors. They should be encouraged, if these feelings are prolonged and severe, to contact their GP or school counsellor.

Try asking young people if they have felt 'down' from time to time. If you are doing this in a group, the group will realize that this is normal and most young people have experienced this. Ask them what sorts of things make them feel sad and what sorts of things make them feel better.

The following can make young people feel depressed: their parents arguing, their parents separating, someone they know committing suicide, someone they know becoming very ill, falling out with a close friend, feeling too much pressure to achieve, feeling unable to cope, being bullied or feeling unattractive. Other causes include experiences of abuse, racism or poverty, difficulties around adoption, or fostering issues or addiction problems.

When these things happen at once, young people may find it more difficult to cope and will feel depressed for a while. They may not know why they feel sad. They may feel depression, anger, stress, pressure, fear, loneliness, confusion, guilt, shame, or a combination of these feelings. Feeling sad is an important response to things in our life or things going on in our mind. It can tell us that something is not right in our life or in the way we are thinking about our life, and we can use this as a sign to do something to improve this.

The key to recovery is to be aware that we are not happy and to do something about it. By doing something positive or talking to someone about the way we feel, we can definitely start to improve things. This is often difficult when we feel down, as life seems pointless and without hope. Depression can make it difficult to see the different options that are open to us. We find it hard to see that there are things we can do to make ourselves feel better.

It is sometimes hard to assess whether young people are depressed or just feeling down. This is important to know in order to help them to decide what action to take. It is a question of the intensity, duration and cause of the feelings (if they know), and the impact they are having on their day-to-day functioning.

Depression can mean feeling extremely sad or just numb. It is increasingly common in young people. It is likely that today's young people are experiencing more pressures, expectations and disappointments than in the past. They may feel increasingly isolated, as there seem to be fewer people, systems and beliefs they can rely on and life seems to change so quickly. They may feel that it is assumed they can cope with a great deal of changes and stressful situations alone. When young people encounter problems, they need stability and adults to rely on. They need people to support them, to help them to understand what they are going through and help them feel better.

The symptoms of depression are listed below. Try asking young people to think of these first.

Depression affects:

- *The way we think*. We believe we deserve the worst, blame ourselves for everything, see everything as meaningless, feel things will always be this way and can never improve, focus continually on problems, failures and negative feelings, hate oneself, lose interest in life and other people, have thoughts of harming oneself, and find it hard to concentrate and make decisions.
- *The way we feel*. We feel sad and unhappy, numb, hopeless, worthless, unattractive, helpless, irritable, tense, anxious and worried, guilty, as if we can't cope with things, under pressure, low in self-confidence and self-esteem, we take no pleasure out of anything, and we feel no sense of mastery or achievement.
- *The way we behave*. We do less, everything seems like a huge effort, we find it hard to get out of bed in the morning, we withdraw from meeting people socially or at work, we feel restless, we sigh and cry a lot.

- *Our physical well-being.* We eat, drink, sleep and smoke a lot more or less than usual. We may find ourselves waking early in the morning in a very low mood. We feel lethargic and exhausted.

What can young people do?
Talk about it

The most important thing, if we are experiencing these symptoms, is to express our feelings. Sometimes just talking about the way we feel to an understanding person can make us feel better. Research has shown that having someone to listen to us and help us to talk through what we're feeling is of huge benefit when we feel sad.

We can also express how we feel in other ways. Keeping a diary, painting or writing songs, poetry or short stories are examples of things that can help us to work through what has happened or is happening, and to reflect on what this means and often what we need to do to move on. They also allow us to express feelings we wouldn't want to share with others. We don't always feel the benefits immediately, but they usually come with time. Ask young people how they let off steam, if they find it hard to talk about feelings of sadness, what the obstacles might be, what might help them feel more comfortable, if it is harder for young men to talk about their feelings, if they keep a diary and to discuss their reasons.

If they're cynical about the positive benefits, suggest they experiment next time they feel down by choosing an understanding person whom they trust to talk to, and to think about how they feel afterwards. The best person is someone whom they find easy to talk to. Friends, brothers, sisters, parents, teachers, aunts, uncles, grandparents, GPs or counsellors can be very helpful in making them feel happier. It is important that they communicate the depth and duration of their feelings, so that these people will take them seriously as well as choosing an appropriate time to commence the discussion. Encourage them to arrange a time that will suit both people to sit down and talk, as they could easily misinterpret inconvenience as disinterest if they pick a bad time for this other person.

Young people are often unaware of how many of their peers feel the same way, and so talking to friends can be a useful source of support. You can also mention the availability of a counsellor at school if there is one. You can also provide them with a list of phone numbers and addresses of local and national help agencies (such as Childline or the Samaritans) and details of any school facilities.

Use their support systems

Many things may stop young people discussing their feelings with others. They may feel ashamed or worried about finding out the worst. They may feel weak and that they are to blame for their feelings of depression.

Next time they feel depressed, ask them to remember that support will help them through it by showing them:

- that someone cares about them
- that other people have felt and feel the same way
- that these problems have been experienced by others
- why they are depressed and the problems in life which have made them feel down
- different and more realistic perspectives
- different solutions to problems.

Sharing problems with friends will also help them to do what is necessary to feel better. We need this help because depression can destroy our energy and motivation. Although there are many potential causes of depression, as well as talking to people we trust or seeking professional help, there are things that we ourselves can do to improve the way we feel. We need to look at the things we do, the way we think and the people in our life.

Young people who suffer from depression need hope and help. You need to encourage them to start by concentrating on small changes, to move them in the right direction away from their depression. This means focusing on the next step and trying not to look too far ahead. They need to make their goal simply feeling better. They won't feel marvellous straight away, but focusing on small changes in the way they think and behave will allow the process of feeling better to begin.

Ways of alleviating depression

These include:

- *Increasing what we do.* Although depression deprives us of energy and makes us feel very tired, setting ourselves small tasks is the first step towards feeling better. Doing small things like going for a walk or phoning a friend can help to lift our mood. Completing tasks helps bring a sense of mastery and pleasure.
- *Thought catching.* Young people need to be aware of their self-talk. This is probably making them feel worse and telling them they will never feel better. Once they are aware of this they can start challenging these statements. When we are sad, we

tend to remember sad times and appraise things more negatively. If they need to analyse what is happening in their lives, it is best to wait until their mood lifts to begin this.

- *Reality check.* If they can remember when they are feeling like this, that their perspective is distorted, this might help them to view things more clearly and prevent them from feeling even worse.

- *Switch off.* When there is nothing we can do to change a situation, it is often useful to just switch off. Going to the cinema, playing sport or just trying to have a chat about something else can give our minds a chance to switch off. This can give us the energy we need to recharge and start tackling the problem.

- *Be specific.* Feeling depressed makes us look at things in a very apathetic way and this can perpetuate these feelings. Suggest that young people try instead to think of positive things in specific terms; for example, instead of saying 'I've still got friends', name a friend or some friends and list specific things they have enjoyed or been through, or specific plans that involve both or all of them in the future. The most likely mistake that we can make when we are depressed is mistaking feelings for facts. Thinking or feeling things doesn't make them true.

- *The talking cure.* Talking to others helps in many ways. It is good to know there is somebody else who knows what you're going through and who cares. It can also help you to explore why you are depressed and what sorts of things in your life have been getting you down. A friend can help you think of ways of tackling these problems and will also have a more accurate perspective on your problems and on you than you do yourself. Telling someone else will also mean that you have someone to motivate you and to help you take on the activities which will help you feel better.

Thoughts of harming themselves

When depressed, young people may have thoughts of harming themselves. This is quite common. It does not mean that they are 'going mad', but you do need to take such thoughts seriously. If you mention to young people that this symptom is not uncommon, they are perhaps more likely to feel that they can tell someone about these thoughts and/or behaviours. Encourage them to discuss these thoughts with an adult whom they trust. They should not be afraid of how others will react. Young people are often reluctant to mention their thoughts for fear that others will disapprove, or fail to understand, or for fear that talking about them may actually make them easier to put into effect. In fact, talking about thoughts of harming yourself usually brings some relief. If they feel like putting these into effect, or making plans, they should seek help at once and talk to someone about how they feel.

How to help prevent depression

Because the causes of depression are multifarious, taking preventive steps will not rule out the possibility of young people suffering depression. Genetic, biochemical and sociological factors may determine this outcome. Anyone can get depressed, and they should not feel it is their fault or responsibility if they do. There are, however, certain basic preventive measures that may reduce the likelihood of becoming depressed.

HELPING TO PREVENT DEPRESSION

Encourage young people to:

- Get enough *sleep* – this will help them to feel on top of things and able to cope, and will also keep their mood positive.

- Remember that *drinking* may make them feel good for a while, but it is often followed by a low. Alcohol is a depressant. It can also help distract them from problems which should really be confronted and resolved.

- Eat well – not *eating* enough will make them feel irritable, depressed, tired and weak. Girls in particular are under a lot of pressure these days to stay slim. Eating a balanced diet will help them stay healthy, in a good mood and give them energy. All these things will help them to enjoy life to the full.

- Get enough *exercise* – this is one of the best ways of staying in good form. If they do start feeling down, it can help to alleviate these feelings and give them a boost.

- Make room for things they *enjoy* – these will help keep them happy!

- Spend time developing good *relationships* – so that they have people to turn to when they feel down.

It is also important to *lead a balanced life*. It is normal for us all to have times when things in one area of our lives are not going as well as they should (e.g. our homework, school, family relationships, or problems with friends or boyfriends/girlfriends). If all our happiness is bound into one of these areas we will be very vulnerable if things go wrong with that aspect of our lives. If, for example, our self-esteem depends on our being part of a couple, breaking up might make it feel as if the world is coming to an end. Similarly, if our school work is the most important thing in our life we may suffer extreme exam nerves and stress, as all our eggs are in this basket. It is therefore a good idea to have several parts to our life: school, family, friends, hobbies, interests and so on. Then, at times when one part of our life is not going according to plan, we can get pleasure and comfort from another part.

Worry and anxiety

Worrying is a vicious circle, as it just makes us feel more wound up and anxious. It puts us in a bad mood and drains us of energy. Most of the things we worry about never happen, or are not as bad as we thought they would be. Even when things turn out for the worst, worrying has rarely helped to achieve anything, and may even leave us feeling less able to cope when it happens.

Try asking young people to think of something they have been worried about. Has this worrying helped resolve the difficulty? How does worrying affect thinking, behaviour, feelings or physical well-being?

What worrying achieves

Worrying is only useful if it makes us aware of something that needs to be remedied, allows us to resolve the situation and move on. It is bad for us when it constantly fills our mind and we take no action or remain preoccupied. It wastes time and energy.

Worrying interferes with our ability to concentrate and to focus on other things, it makes it hard to take decisions and makes us concentrate on negative aspects of situations. It is also a habit that we can learn to break. When we're worrying, we pay less attention to the task at hand and so our work can suffer, and it can also make us feel less confident as well as confused, anxious and helpless. Physically, when we are worried, we lose our ability to relax and sleep properly. We can get tired and run down. It can give us headaches and make us feel tense.

How to get rid of worries[3]

Suggest that young people divide their worries into (1) those they can do something about, and (2) those they can't do anything about. For the first category, they should decide whether they can do something about it now or later, and plan to act on that. The second category includes all worries that are unimportant, unlikely or unresolved. Unimportant worries are those which they can't see themselves worrying about in five years' time or things which simply aren't worth the worry. Unlikely worries are those which are probably never going to happen. Finally, there is no point worrying about things which are unresolved. They should wait to see what happens and then decide what to do.

SUMMARY

There are only two choices when we find ourselves worrying:

1 Use a problem-solving approach and do something about it.
2 Stop worrying about it.

This advice might seem easier said than done. The following tips will help young people to banish worrying.

- *Distraction*. You can only pay full attention to one thing at a time. When we are busy we have less time to worry. It's important, however, not to misuse distraction as a way of avoiding the task of thinking about problems. If there is something young people can do, they should use problem-solving strategies to try to solve it.
- *Only in the daytime*. The middle of the night is often when our worries loom large and seem most disturbing. Encourage young people to ban night-time worrying. They should be disciplined with themselves and insist as soon as a worry pops into their head that 'This is not the time'. They can write down their worries and forget about them until morning, try visualizing a pleasant image, or try a relaxation exercise, such as progressive relaxation described in Chapter 3.
- *Back in their box*. Suggest that they think of their own image for dispensing with the worry, for example, putting their worries in a box and closing the lid. If they need to remember it they can write it down.

- *Fence them in*. If worrying is a major problem, you could suggest that young people even put aside a regular half-hour each day to worry. This will stop their days and nights being plagued by worrying. It can also help worrying to turn into problem-solving and thus become more productive.

Worries are usually false predictions

People often believe they are worried about something they have said and done. However, the root cause of the anxiety is usually a prediction about the way this will affect the future or about being unable to cope in the future. Worrying can be alleviated if you can encourage young people to examine these predictions and challenge them.

- *Question assumptions*. Ask them to think about what they are really worried about. Is it really about having offended a friend by not telephoning, or are they more concerned that they will be rejected too readily by that person? Challenging these assumptions will allow them to take apart the worrying messages they send out.
- *Talk about it*. As with feelings of stress and depression, discussing their worries will give them the support, advice and relief often necessary to discard those worries. Other people can ask questions to help them identify what the worry is about, and can offer different and often more realistic perspectives. They can also practise asking themselves the questions they want to ask someone else, and try to answer them themselves. This can encourage self-reliance and self-confidence in young people.

CONCLUSION

In order to manage stress effectively, young people need to value themselves, and so this chapter discussed ways of boosting self-confidence and self-esteem. In addition, depression and anxiety may arise through poor coping skills, or may be a source of stress in the lives of young people. It was suggested that you discuss:

- treats or sources of energy

- what self-confidence is, where it comes from and how to increase it

- what self-esteem is, where it comes from and how to boost it
- the symptoms of depression
- ways of coping with depression
- ways of preventing depression
- thoughts of self-harm
- how to limit worry and anxiety.

Notes

1 Butler, G. and Hope, T. (1995) *The Mental Fitness Guide: Manage Your Mind.* Oxford: Oxford University Press.
2 Ibid.
3 Ibid.

CHAPTER 7

Discussion and conclusion

Introduction
This chapter seeks to (1) summarize the aims of the book, (2) highlight important points to remember when instigating programmes for stress reduction, (3) discuss the role of socioeconomic factors, (4) summarize advice on stress management for young people, and (5) place stress interventions in the context of a changing world.

The aim of the book
This book aims to give those working with or in contact with young people the necessary information, techniques and ideas to discuss the issue of stress and suggest ways in which young people can cope better with the stress in their lives. It provides practical advice about raising pertinent issues and relating useful coping strategies to teenagers.

Chapter 1 gave advice on location and tone when discussing stress with young people. It discussed issues of confidentiality, role changes, ownership and gender issues. It was recommended that young people be encouraged to talk about sources of stress in their lives, resources, and symptoms and outcomes of stress as well as the benefits of learning to cope more effectively with stress.

Chapter 2 focused on mental ways of coping with stress. Fundamental to this discussion was exploring the link between events, thoughts and feelings. It was recommended that young people be encouraged to keep a stress diary to explore the relationship between their internal self-talk and feelings of strain and worry. Appraisal was identified as playing a key role in the maintenance of stress-related symptoms. Advice was given on learning to plan ahead, preparing for stressful events, keeping things in perspective, thought stopping, coping skills training, learning how to relax, problem-solving, the importance of humour and different coping strategies.

Because good physical health plays a key protective role in the stress process, Chapter 3 provided information on nutrition, exercise, sleep, breathing, relaxation and the effects of alcohol consumption. Dieting can cause a great deal of stress to the body and make it difficult to cope with normal everyday demands. It was suggested that assumptions around body shape were explored. Advice was also presented on coping with premenstrual syndrome. Key to this chapter was teaching young people about the effect of their physical health on the way they perceive situations, i.e. whether they feel they can cope.

Many young people find it difficult to cope with the stress which arises from exam situations. Chapter 4 provided advice on study skills and time management. First, however, a discussion was recommended on assumptions around achievement and well-being. Young people should be encouraged to discuss the pressure they feel they are under with regard to succeeding. The effects on concentration of diet and physical activity were discussed. Advice was also provided on note-taking and exam preparation.

Learning how to manage relationships well is an important skill in stress management, as they provide much needed support at difficult times in our lives. Chapter 5 aimed to facilitate discussion around the meaning and role of relationships in the lives of young people. It encouraged them to use these relationships as a resource, and also to accept their responsibilities for maintaining the relationship. Young people were encouraged to look for patterns in the way they relate to others which might be rooted in the past. Advice on assertiveness, negotiation and listening skills was provided. Coping with bullying was also discussed.

Chapter 6 presented advice around nurturing and sustaining self-confidence and self-esteem. It also looked at depression and ways it can be understood, prevented or alleviated. It is important that young people recognize the symptoms of depression and are aware of basic recommended courses of action. These include talking to people they trust, and making initial small changes in their thinking or behaviour. A discussion on thoughts of self-harm was also provided. Finally, some basic techniques for conquering worrying were presented.

Programme implementation

In the words of Black and Frauenknecht:

> primary prevention stress-management programs for asymptom-atic adolescents are currently non-existent, although sorely

needed to alleviate detrimental effects of excessive stress. (Black and Frauenknecht, 1990, p. 89)

The majority of evaluative studies which examine the effects of interventions in adolescence are non-comparative by design. The effects of a stress management course with a lecture-discussion format compared to a skills-based course (which incorporated biofeedback training) have been evaluated. Participants on the former programme demonstrated greater reductions in anxiety and subjective stress. Stress management programmes which include problem-solving, coping skills, cognitive skills and general life discussion have all demonstrated significant efficacy in alleviating adolescent distress.

Perhaps the most well-known and widely used stress management programme is Meichenbaum's stress inoculation training. This programme has been used with some success with young people, and incorporates relaxation, cognitive restructuring and assertiveness training. The *Stress Management Programme for Secondary School Students* (McNamara, 2000) has also demonstrated long-term benefits in participants.

Many studies examine differential outcomes in treatment and control groups, but fail to include comparative interventions. It is therefore difficult to dismiss in these studies the potential influence of core or non-specific elements which are shared by any intervention. These include rapport with the participant, suggestion, expectation of relief, treatment credibility and compliance. In other words, people taking part in a course would expect to feel better for doing so, and this expectation may lead to an improvement in symptoms. Shared elements such as an organizational acknowledgement of adolescent difficulties and issues, taking time out, relaxing, space to reflect, sharing experiences, social support and peer counselling are extremely important components for interventions with young people. These are the basics on which further skills and information are layered.

Following extensive research on happiness and well-being, and a review of mood induction and cognitive therapies, Argyle and Martin (1995) recommend that interventions which would enhance well-being should incorporate four components. These are 'persuading people to make different attributions for good and bad events, trying to change the content of ruminations, and increasing optimism and self-esteem' (p. 96).

Furthermore, an intervention study can only show that it has achieved more than general relaxation effects by its strict adherence to the stringent design desiderata proposed by such authors as Stiles *et al.*, who urge that future research should include a

> combination of greater specification of treatment components, via manualization and dismantling strategies, with greater differentiation of outcome measurement, via behavioral assessment and other measurement of specific therapeutic effects. (Stiles *et al.*, 1986, p. 171)

This means that until we have strong research designs which isolate the different components of interventions, we will not know which components are effective over and beyond the non-specific elements listed above.

The importance of accurate assessment is reiterated in an important publication, edited by Takanishi and Hamburg (1997), in which Hamburg writes: 'without credible evidence of benefit, we cannot be sure that the adolescents are receiving the help they need' (p. 130). Six key dimensions to successful programme implementation and assessment are outlined by Hamburg.

The first of these refers to adequate assessment of the specific needs of the target population. Second, selection of an appropriate programme site is discussed in terms of accessibility, acceptance and adequacy of space. A school can be an appropriate forum. Considerable attention should be devoted to choosing an appropriate location within each school which would best facilitate these criteria. For young people who are not attending school, more informal locations such as youth cafés or youth centres may be preferable.

Third, Hamburg discusses the importance of the relationship between the 'action researcher' and the system through which the intervention is to be delivered. The relationship between service providers and the researcher should be highly reciprocal. Detailed feedback reports should be presented at regular intervals to service providers and (when appropriate) to students. Course materials should be made available for school use and talks provided for parents, teachers and students on stress and its effects, complete with book lists, address lists and information handouts.

A fourth recommendation is the provision of manuals for the use of trainers or teachers. Hamburg also refers to procedures for data collection and the importance of securing an adequate information management system. Data collection in real-life settings is always a difficult component of applied research. Every attempt should, however, be made to standardize and maximize data collection. Finally, Hamburg recommends a multi-method, multi-measure approach to evaluation. Evaluation of these interventions should combine self-report ratings with independent ratings and objective data.

Research into the development of stress reduction programmes is increasing but differs on four major dimensions, namely in its focus on individual or environmental change, its focus on specific or general stressors, the types of skills taught, and the emphasis on competency enhancement or problem prevention. This book has focused on individual-based, general stress management, incorporating a variety of coping skills aimed at competency enhancement in an asymptomatic adolescent population. It is also important to examine ways in which the effects of such a programme would be enhanced by (1) the simultaneous delivery of such a course to parents and teachers, (2) tackling environmental stressors identified by the community as stressful to young people, (3) delivering the course to populations which differ in their exposure to risk, and (4) continuing to dismantle treatment components so as to retain only key components with proven efficacy.

More research is required to identify individual and group differences which might influence programme success in order to provide the most appropriate programmes to groups of young people from different backgrounds. Programmes which seek to reduce adolescent distress by improving school environments appear to represent a fruitful and worthy avenue for future research.[1]

The socioeconomic dimension to research

The socioeconomic dimension to this type of research merits comment. Much of the research on risk and resilience, together with the literature on primary prevention, suggests that interventions such as these should target individuals who are at a social or economic disadvantage. However, although school representatives and service providers may be highly enthusiastic about the opportunity this kind of research affords, many of these schools are unable to set aside time for the facilitation of the programmes. When students are invited to take part in the courses after school time, a low response rate may follow, making the provision of courses in these schools unfeasible. Many students at these schools have part-time jobs or are obliged to take care of younger siblings. Therefore, inclusion of stress management within the outlined curriculum is necessary to introduce many of these skills to young people in a formal setting.

More information on socioeconomic status, age and race is needed to identify the different types of stress, ways of coping, moderating factors and outcomes in different populations. It is likely that while generic stresses, such as negotiating transitions, familial conflicts, goal attainment and relationship formation, are general across all groups, other sources of stress will be relevant to young people from different geographical, educational, social and economic backgrounds. More research is needed on the types of stress management projects which are most effective with different populations.

There are also many societal changes required to alleviate stress in young people. These include, among others, changes in education and training, improved counselling and psychological services, continued research on youth needs, programme evaluation and policy change, a continued focus on children's rights, improved recreational facilities, drugs awareness programmes, economic policies and legislation which support children and families, nurturing educational environments, pro-youth urban planning, and good childcare facilities. In summary, we should be supporting young people through adequate education, physical and mental healthcare together with family, economic and social support. Young people also need to be afforded more flexible trajectories which allow them to develop and feel included and respected through alternative routes in education, training and employment.

Young people may be under stress because of structural inequalities, racial prejudice, where they live and other socioeconomic factors. It is clear that stress management is not going to undermine societal pressures which militate against all young people getting the same advantages in life. However, teaching people how to feel self-confident, how to look after their mental and physical health, how to learn efficiently and, most importantly, to discuss issues which are upsetting them will give them highly important skills. Discussing issues in a group setting with their peers will teach them that many young people share similar problems and difficulties. They will also learn that things which are relatively easy for them may be highly stressful for others.

OVERVIEW OF STRESS MANAGEMENT FOR YOUNG PEOPLE

Of the many suggestions contained in this book, in order to help them to manage their stress levels it is recommended that young people should:

- Use their *support networks* and talk about difficulties as they emerge.

- Be aware of *people* or *organizations* that they can talk to about specific problems.

- Lead a *balanced lifestyle* which has varied components (e.g. school, family, friends, homework, leisure, hobbies, recreation, rest and time alone).

- Get lots of *exercise*, particularly aerobic exercise. They can try walking, running, cycling, swimming or dancing. A brisk walk when they are studying or before an exam will help them to think more clearly and improve their memory.

- Eat a *healthy diet* and avoid too much caffeine, sugar and fats. This causes internal stress and makes us more irritable, tired and likely to feel that we can't cope. Foods which contain carbohydrates, like pasta, bread, potatoes and cereal, act as natural tranquillizers to help us feel calm. Getting enough vitamins from fruit and vegetables also helps us to stay healthy and increase our capacity to cope.

- Try some *relaxation* every day or when they feel stressed. They will need a quiet place, to be sitting upright, with good posture, and deep breathing. If they suffer from stress, they should get into the habit of doing breathing, stretching and relaxation exercises regularly.

- Get enough *sleep*. Young people need up to nine hours a night and should try to get into good sleep routines.

- Remember the importance of *appraisal*: to feel stressed we must interpret things as a threat and assume that we do not have the resources to deal with the demands. We can use coping skills, relaxation, positive appraisal, problem-solving, and remember our social and personal resources.

- Utilize *good study skills*, which basically involves remaining calm, focused and organized.

- Manage their *time* so that they divide it up between the things that are important to them. Try to get straight down to work so that they don't spend time hanging around feeling guilty and unsettled. Get it over and done with and then relax.

- When they feel stressed, they need to try to identify exactly what it is that is bothering them, then treat it as a *problem* in need of a *solution*. They should think of as many solutions as possible and work out which one they would like to try first. If this doesn't work, move on to the next solution and so on.

- Be aware of the sorts of things that give them *energy* (e.g. friends, exercise, food, laughing) and the sorts of things that drain energy (e.g. depression, lack of exercise, feeling a loss of control, arguments) so that they can try to reduce those that drain energy.

- Try to remember their *resources* as well as the demands they face. These include people in their life, and things about them that they like (e.g. their sense of humour, a feeling of confidence in certain things or a hobby that they have).

- Try to keep things in perspective, think *positively* and have a sense of humour about life.

- Remember that the *people* they care about who could help them when stressed are often the people they are most likely to attack. They should try not to take it out on others when stressed so that these people will be there to help them when they need them.

- Remember that being *assertive* means being fair to oneself and to others.

Conclusion

A consensus exists that today's young people are experiencing more distress than the youth of previous generations. This is evident in increasing rates of stress, suicide, depression, eating disorders, anxiety and drug use. No such consensus exists regarding the optimum preventive strategy which would successfully combat these trends. Researchers on adolescent stress are generally in favour of the development of stress reduction interventions. Johnson writes:

> a major task for the future will be the development of inter-vention programmes for helping children cope with stressful events. Although preliminary work in this area has been carried out, the development of such coping skills programmes largely remains a challenge for the future. (Johnson, 1982, p. 250)

Others agree, arguing that the 'development of effective and powerful prevention strategies is necessary'[2] and that the need for health education and life skills training, both now and in the foreseeable future, is so compelling that it should be as universal as possible.[3]

The implications of the issues discussed in this book are important. First, with regard to adolescent mental health rates, research suggests that adolescents comprise, on average, one in three of all psychiatric referrals.[4] This book argues that adolescent distress may be significantly reduced by learning skills in stress management. Second, we need to think about the way in which we are preparing young people for predicted changes in the job market. The impact of these changes on mental health is a highly pertinent research area for psychology. Research supports the relationship between long-term unemployment and mental health problems, such as depression and low self-esteem. Conversely, within the workforce there is also a growing concern regarding levels of stress, with the Royal College of General Practitioners in the UK calling for the teaching of 'stress-proofing' skills to avoid burnout within the work environment.

This book is important given the dearth of both formal and informal resources for practitioners in helping young people to cope with stress. Many of the skills included have been shown to bolster self-esteem and improve academic performance and well-being while reducing anxiety. It is argued, therefore, that learning these skills in school would increase the competency of young people to cope with stress both in the job market and in periods of unemployment.

It is further argued that stress management training may address the lacuna within intervention research whereby interventions focus exclusively on either personal competencies or the social environment. Stress management training appears to ameliorate individual resources by teaching effective coping strategies while enhancing the environment through the improved social resources provided by group meetings and received training in social skills.

It is argued that the inclusion of stress reduction programmes within the school curriculum can successfully buffer adolescents against present and future stressors. These conclusions have far-reaching policy implications. The World Health Organization (WHO) has supported life skills education within schools and has published two important documents presenting the rationale, conceptual base and course materials for life skills training.[5] This is indicative of the scale of recognition which now exists regarding the need for competence enhancement and skills training in schools.

An imbalance remains, however, regarding this recognition on the one hand, and the lack of resources or methodologically sound evaluation studies of appropriate interventions on the other. This book aims to provide those working with young people, and in a position to implement programmes on stress management, with guidelines around implementation and evaluation. It is hoped that in so doing it redresses this imbalance and provides a useful guide to supporting teenagers through this crucial and difficult life stage, as well as providing them with skills that will remain with them throughout life.

It is time to prioritize the needs of young people and to acknowledge that current levels of stress are unacceptable. Together with providing a safer, more supportive and challenging environment for today's youth, we can take the knowledge provided by research and our experiences of working with young people and teach them skills that will stay with them throughout the exciting future that lies ahead.

Notes

1 Comer, J. (1991) 'The Comer School Development Program'. *Urban Education*, **26**, 56–82.

2 DuBois, D. L., Felner, R. D., Brand, S., Adan, A. M. and Evans, E. G. (1992) 'A prospective study of life stress, social support, and adaptation in early adolescence'. *Child Development*, **63**, 542–57 (p. 542).

3 Hamburg, B. (1990) *Life Skills Training: Preventive Interventions for Young Adolescents*. New York: Carnesis Council on Adolescent Development.

4 Houlihan, B., Fitzgerald, M. and O'Regan, M. (1994) 'Self-esteem, depression and hostility in Irish adolescents'. *Journal of Adolescence*, **17**(6), 565–77.

5 'Part I: Introduction to life skills for psychosocial competence' and 'Part II: Guidelines: the development and implementation of life skills programmes' issued by the Division of Mental Health of the World Health Organization.

References

Chapter 1
Whelan, D. (1993) *Your Breaking Point: Effective Steps to Reduce and Cope with Stress*. Dublin: Attic Press.

Chapter 2
Ellis, A. (1984) 'The place of meditation in rational-emotive therapy and cognitive-behavior therapy', in D. H. Shapiro and R. N. Walsh (eds) *Meditation: Classic and Contemporary Perspectives*. New York: Aldin.

Chapter 6
Whelan, D. (1993) *Your Breaking Point: Effective Steps to Reduce and Cope with Stress*. Dublin: Attic Press.

Chapter 7
Argyle, M. and Martin, M. (1995) 'Testing for stress and happiness: the role of social and cognitive factors', in C. D. Spielberger and I. G. Sarason (eds) *Stress and Emotion, Vol. 15*, pp. 173–87. Washington, DC: Taylor and Francis.

Argyle, M., Martin, M. and Crossland, J. (1989) 'Happiness as a function of personality and social factors', in J. P. Forgas and J. M. Innes (eds) *Recent Advances in Social Psychology: An International Perspective*. Elsevier Science Publishers B. V. North Holland.

Black, D. R. and Frauenknecht, M. (1990) 'A primary prevention problem-solving program for adolescent stress management', in *Human Stress, Current Selected Research, 4*, pp. 89–109. New York: AMS Press.

Johnson, J. H. (1982) 'Life events as stressors in childhood and adolescence', in B. Lahey and F. Kazdin (eds) *Advances in Clinical Child Psychology*, pp. 220–50. London: Plenum Press.

McNamara, S. (2000) *Stress Management Programme for Secondary School Students*. London: Routledge.

Stiles, W. B., Shapiro, D. A. and Firth-Cozens, J. A. (1988) 'Do sessions of different treatments have different impacts?' *Journal of Counseling Psychology, 35*(4), 391–6.

Stiles, W. B., Shapiro, D. A. and Elliott, R. (1986) 'Are all psychotherapies equivalent?' *American Psychologist, 41*(2), 165–80.

Takanishi, R. and Hamburg, D. A. (eds) (1997) *Preparing Adolescents for the Twenty-first Century: Challenges Facing Europe and the US*. Cambridge: Cambridge University Press.